The Effective Correctional Officer

American Correctional Association

Perry M. Johnson, President
James A. Gondles, Jr., Executive Director
Patricia L. Poupore, Director of Communications and Publications
Elizabeth Watts, Publications Managing Editor
Marianna Nunan, Project Editor
Kristen M. Miller, Editorial Assistant
Karen C. Ruhren, Contributing Editor

ISBN 0-929310-64-0

Printed in the United States of America by BookCrafters,
Fredericksburg, Va.

American Correctional Association
8025 Laurel Lakes Court
Laurel, MD 20707-5075

Contents

Foreword

Today's correctional officers face many challenges. The constantly changing environment of corrections makes increasing demands on correctional officers, who must tap into the few resources available to them to successfully meet those demands. *The Effective Correctional Officer* is one such resource; it addresses issues of concern to correctional officers.

Both officers who have served corrections for many years and those new to the field will find the articles on ethics on the job, role ambiguity, styles of control and supervision, racial differences and supervising inmates, avoiding manipulation, hostage situations, and supervising special needs inmates helpful in performing their everyday duties competently and professionally. These articles offer solid, practical information.

Those contemplating a career in corrections as a correctional officer will find special meaning in articles like "Career vs. Job: Why Become a Correctional Officer?" and "Moving Ahead in Your Career."

The correctional officer's job involves more than simply following rules and regulations and policies and procedures. Interactions with inmates are unpredictable. As a result correctional officers are always under a high degree of stress. Articles on wellness, staff substance abuse, correctional officers and their families dealing with stress, and how to handle litigation provide information that will prepare officers to cope with the daily challenges of the job.

Supervising inmates can be a tough job, but correctional officers who conduct themselves as professionals will find a career in corrections rewarding. The correctional officer has a critical role in achieving corrections' goal of protecting the public and in helping offenders improve their lives. The American Correctional Association recognizes the importance of the correctional officer and is dedicated to serving their needs and providing resources like *The Effective Correctional Officer* to maximize their effectiveness.

The American Correctional Association wishes to thank all the authors who contributed to this book, many who contributed freely of their time and professional expertise. We are also grateful to those individuals who acted as reviewers and advisors in the editing of this book, particularly Dr. Joann B. Morton.

James A. Gondles, Jr.
Executive Director
American Correctional Association

Career vs. Job: Why Become a Correctional Officer?

By The Honorable Helen G. Corrothers

> *When I look back on the processes of history, when I survey the genesis of America, I see this written over every page: that the nations are renewed from the bottom, not from the top; that the genius which springs up from the ranks of unknown men is the genius which renews the youth and energy of the people. Everything I know about history, every bit of experience and observation that has contributed to my thought, has confirmed me in the conviction that the real wisdom of human life is compounded out of the experiences of ordinary men. . . . The great struggling unknown masses of the men who are at the base of everything are the dynamic force that is lifting the levels of society. A nation is as great, and only as great, as her rank and file.*
>
> *Woodrow Wilson, 1914*

There is no field of endeavor more exciting and challenging than criminal justice and no component with more opportunities to "make a difference" than corrections. However, to paraphrase Woodrow Wilson: Corrections is as great, and only as great, as its employees. Among its employees, we find correctional officers, who have tremendous responsibilities and therefore tremendous opportunities to ensure the correctional mission is achieved.

Those who work in corrections, or any other field, must decide whether their work constitutes a job or a career. It is

The Honorable Helen G. Corrothers is former president of the American Correctional Association and a former commissioner on the U.S. Sentencing Commission.

1

important to recognize the differences and to know how to make the transition from a job to a career.

The difference in one word is *commitment.* When you have a career, you are committed to your organization's goals and objectives, and your performance of assigned tasks or functions is enhanced by that sense of commitment and dedication. Successful supervisors foster employees' commitment to the organization's goals. Successful employees internalize that commitment and make it a part of their personal goals and objectives, thereby making the transition from a job to a career.

Obviously, it takes a lot less effort to have a job than to have a career. However, the effort put into developing a career pays off in terms of personal growth and fulfillment, as well as financial status.

Why pursue a career as a correctional officer? In answering this question, several factors should be considered: the need for more correctional officers, the significance of the correctional officer's role in achieving major correctional goals and objectives, and the pride and self-esteem of being a correctional officer.

The Need for More Correctional Officers

The criminal justice system as a whole is overburdened. As a result, the business of corrections is perhaps this country's fastest growing industry.

Statistics released in 1991 by the federal Bureau of Justice Statistics (BJS) reflect an increase in the use of probation. "The nation's probation population increased 5.9 percent last year to 2.67 million, and the parole population rose 16.3 percent to more than 530,000."

According to a BJS study, the prison population continues to increase—in 1991, the population in federal and state prisons rose 6.2 percent, reaching a new high of 823,000. The increase indicated a need for 900 prison beds per week last year. The country's jail population is also at an all-time high of 426,476 as of mid-1991 (*Corrections Today* 1992). In 1991 "more than 12,000 state prisoners were being held in local jails or other facilities because of crowding in state institutions" (*Criminal Justice Newsletter* 1991).

A 1991 study indicated that "the criminal justice system of the United States has produced the world's highest known rate of incarceration" (*Criminal Justice Newsletter* 1991), with 426 jail and prison inmates per 100,000 people. Despite our willingness to incarcerate, the violent crime rate continues to climb. The FBI reported that the number of violent crimes increased 5 percent in 1991 (*Criminal Justice Newsletter* 1992). American taxpayers are unhappy because of increasing fear of crime and frustrated that the system is not more successful.

The media have focused on the price tag for our policies, which ranges from $16 billion to $20 billion per year, depending on your source. Prison cell construction can cost as much as $100,000, and operational costs can amount to $30,000 per inmate per year. In May 1992, Attorney General Barr cited average construction costs of $53,000 per bed and operations costs of $21,000 per inmate per year. The media seem more concerned about the number of offenders and the related costs than how the numbers relate to the demands put on the correctional system and the officers who work in the system. It is obvious that the increase in the number of offenders in our criminal justice system and corrections means there is a concurrent need for an increase in the number of correctional officers serving the system. According to the American Correctional Association, there are approximately 241,700 correctional officers in the country. There is no doubt that there is now and in the foreseeable future a tremendous and urgent need for additional correctional officers.

Correctional Officers' Role in Achieving Corrections' Goal

The significance of the correctional officer's role in the correctional system cannot be fully appreciated without full comprehension of corrections' primary purpose. Unfortunately, there is some confusion on just what that purpose is. The purpose of corrections is no different from that of the other components of the criminal justice system; it is to protect the public. Corrections' goal to protect the public can be achieved through two objectives: (1) prevent escapes and otherwise humanely incarcerate offenders until their lawful release and (2) provide a safe (for both inmates and staff) and appropriate environment that is conducive to influencing offenders to learn and adopt positive and appropriate value systems, thus creating a desire in them to lead productive and law-abiding lives when they are released into the community.

I stand by this strong working definition of the system's primary goal and supporting objectives; however, it is not shared unanimously in the field. Some believe that the effort to rehabilitate is important and worthwhile and should be undertaken but that it conflicts with the law enforcement component's effort to accomplish its mission to protect society. Others believe that the protection of society *is* a correctional goal and that the rehabilitative effort is worthwhile, but that rehabilitation is not directly related to the protection of society and it should be handled by entities outside of corrections. For example, Dr. William E. Amos, former chairman of the Youth Corrections Division of the U.S. Board of Parole believed: "(1) We should confine fewer people. (2) The philosophy of confinement should be deterrence, accountability, and the protection of society—*not rehabilitation.* (3) Adequate training or rehabilitation centers should be operated by *other agencies. . . .*" (Fogel 1975).

I disagree with Dr. Amos and those who share his belief because I see no conflict between the effort to protect society and the effort to rehabilitate—rehabilitation is viewed as an effort to influence a discontinuance of criminal behavior.

Corrections relies on correctional officers to attain its goal and objectives. Tony Travisono, former executive director of the American Correctional Association (ACA), when describing ACA's dedication to serving the needs of correctional officers, said, "Correctional officers can make or break the correctional system, depending on their attitudes and style of supervising and managing inmates. . . . As those who deal directly with inmates, correctional officers have a central, critical role in corrections, with either positive or negative consequences for themselves, inmates, their institutions, and the public. The American Correctional Association is committed to providing support and training for this important segment of the field" (ACA 1983).

Academicians have recognized the abilities of correctional officers as well as the system's dependence on them. Dr. Barry D. Smith (1983), then an assistant professor in the Criminal Justice Department at Southeast Missouri State University, described the position of correctional officer as a "stressful and potentially dangerous occupation, requiring a great deal of skill and adaptability." Referring to the importance of the officers' role in the system, Dr. Smith said, "The 'balance' of any correctional institution depends on many factors; however, the backbone of correctional institutions is the correctional officers and their styles of control and supervision."

The confusion over the purpose of corrections has resulted in the devaluation of the correctional officer's contributions to the system and to society. Gordon Hawkins, in his book *The Prison: Policy and Practice* (1976), agrees that correctional officers have been neglected: "One of the most curious features of the whole history of modern imprisonment is the way the custodial officer, the key figure in the penal equation, the man on whom the whole edifice of the penitentiary depends, has with astonishing consistency either been ignored or traduced or idealized but almost never considered seriously."

Because of this devaluation and the general lack of appreciation for the contributions of corrections (which is reflected in the lack of sufficient public support), I strongly believe better communication with the public is needed to inform them of the purpose of corrections and its accomplishments in meeting its objectives and to promote appreciation and recognition of correctional employees. Indeed, this area has been a major concern during my term as president of ACA. ACA has traditionally offered significant training and technical assistance opportunities to correctional employees. ACA's consensus to increase this focus on correctional employees is expected to influence the nation's correctional agencies to join in more effectively communicating to the public the importance and extent of the system's reliance on correctional officers. Correctional officers can expect a brighter future—a future that will provide them a much improved level of respect and appreciation that they so richly deserve.

Substantial Reasons for Pride

There are substantial reasons to be proud to be a correctional officer. If you think of a train as representing corrections, then corrections administrators who provide leadership and vision are not on the train, but are out in front, "laying track." They give us direction, and they work to acquire the necessary personnel/resources and abilities to get us where we want to go. However, the train needs staff to keep it on the track, and unless we want the train to be motionless, it needs staff to keep it fueled. Will Rogers has said, "Even if you're on the right track, you'll get run over if you just sit there." In the correctional system, correctional officers keep programs on track and fueled. Without them, the system will fail to realize its mission.

Consider this: The most sophisticated security system that modern technology can provide and the best written security policies and procedures cannot ensure meeting the correctional objective of preventing escapes and humanely holding offenders until their lawful release. We rely on correctional employees to carry out security policies and procedures. Indeed, correctional officers' diligence and attention to duty directly correspond to the quality of security of a facility. Corrections' rehabilitative objective can be accomplished only in the appropriate environment—an environment in which inmates feel safe and where rehabilitation is encouraged and supported. The correctional officer's attitude and degree of professionalism contribute to this type of environment.

Correctional officers have the primary responsibility of maintaining security. They also have the most interaction with inmates on a daily basis and therefore the greatest opportunity to influence the attitudinal factors most conducive to rehabilitation.

Discipline is effective when inmates observe correctional officers consistently enforcing rules and regulations in a fair and impartial manner. When inmates perceive discipline as fair and appropriate, they respect authority while they are incarcerated and when they are released.

Program staff are responsible for the quality of risk-reducing programs and inmate motivation; however, they must work with correctional officers in a team effort to ensure the success of these programs. In addition to influencing inmates and encouraging them to participate in worthwhile programs, the duty of correctional officers to provide inmates with a safe environment plays a major role in rehabilitation. No matter how well-developed the program curriculum or how interested and motivated the instructor, inmates will not benefit if they are preoccupied with concerns about personal safety.

In response to the question of the value of the correctional officer, we would have to ask another question, "How valuable is safety to the American public?" Without a doubt, that value is immeasurable; it is a matter of the greatest magnitude and priority. Public safety is America's most precious commodity. A tremendous amount of self-esteem should come from the realization that being a correctional officer means you are in the position to help salvage what would be wasted lives of those inmates who desire rehabilitation. To the extent that rehabilitation is successful, correctional officers have assisted the inmate's family because the family members may now be part of a functional family; they have assisted in reducing the taxpayers' burden because now that the inmate is a productive member of society, he or she will support his or her family; and they have enhanced public safety because now that the inmate is law-abiding, potential victims of crime will be spared. As a correctional officer, you are employed within a system that has the most important mission possible—that of protecting the public. Moreover, corrections needs you, the correctional officer, to meet its primary goal.

Maximizing Your Effectiveness

Looking at Problems as Opportunities

Perhaps doomsayers will remind us of the paucity or lack of literature encouraging you to become a correctional officer. In fact, they could note that when the importance of the correctional officer is mentioned, it is within the context of a discussion of the problems or difficulties of the correctional system.

7

Don't let existing literature dissuade you. A positive attitude in corrections will allow you to see challenges as opportunities— opportunities to expand your imagination, wake up energies, and stir creative juices to help you to develop necessary strategies. When you successfully meet the correctional challenges confronting you, you elevate your self-esteem and experience the sense of self-fulfillment and exhilaration that accompanies an exciting career.

Believing You Can Make a Difference

Although most of us want an interesting and exciting career, we also want to "make a difference." Richard Nelson Bolles (1990), a leading career counselor, writes: "The motive that drives us to search for A Sense of Mission is our desire for some reassurance of our Uniqueness. We want to see that we are not just another grain of sand lying on the beach called humanity, outnumbered and lost in the five billion mass, but that the Universe-God caused us to be born and be put here for some unique reason: to contribute to Life on earth something no one else can contribute in quite the same way. At its very minimum, then, if you search for a sense of Mission you are searching for reassurance that the world is at least a little bit richer for your being here; and a little bit poorer after your going."

I admit to being an eternal optimist. In my "storehouse of tools for life," there is a belief that a positive attitude makes a significant difference and that faith is an important power source. It should be noted that the positive outlook reflected here does not mean that there are not sometimes temporary setbacks in one's career. However, these difficulties should be treated like any other professional challenge. Vince Lombardi had good advice when he said: "It's not whether you get knocked down, it's whether you get up again."

Conclusion

This chapter has been devoted to showing the importance and value of the correctional officer by describing and discussing the significance of the mission of corrections. Additionally, there has been a specific description of how the correctional officer contributes to the accomplishment of each objective deemed essential to the achievement of the overall mission. There has been the effort to show clearly that without the correctional officer, the accomplishment of corrections' goal and objectives is impossible. It is with certainty that we say that, as a correctional officer, you can make a difference.

However successful you become in your career, continue your effort to maximize your effectiveness, never stop growing, never stop improving, continue to "make your best better." Art Linkletter shares this philosophy and has said: "Do a little more than you're paid to; give a little more than you have to; try a little harder than you want to; aim a little higher than you think possible; and give a lot of thanks to God for health, family, and friends."

Corrections is of critical importance to society, therefore as a correctional officer, you are important and valuable. Indeed, you are indispensable to corrections. Feel proud, work hard, and compete with yourself, with how successful you can be. Maximize your effectiveness, join your professional association; maximize your humanity, and know that every day, you make a difference.

References

American Correctional Association. 1992. BJS report. *Corrections Today* 54 (August).

American Correctional Association. 1992. *Juvenile & adult correctional departments, institutions, agencies & paroling authorities directory*. Laurel, Md.: ACA.

American Correctional Association. 1990. *National jail & adult detention directory*. Laurel, Md.: ACA.

Bolles, R. N. 1990. *What color is your parachute? A practical manual for job hunters & career changers*. Berkeley, Calif.: Ten Speed Press.

Criminal Justice Newsletter. 1991. United States leads the world in incarceration, study finds. *Criminal Justice Newsletter* 22 (21).

Criminal Justice Newsletter. 1992. Law enforcement. *Criminal Justice Newsletter* 23 (7).

Fogel, D. 1975. *We are the living proof.* Cincinnati: W. H. Anderson.

Hawkins, G. 1976. *The prison: Policy and practice.* Chicago: University of Chicago Press.

Smith, B. 1983. Styles of control and supervision. In *Correctional officers: Power, pressure and responsibility.* Laurel, Md.: ACA.

Travisono, A. P. 1983. Preface. In *Correctional officers: Power, pressure and responsibility.* Laurel, Md.: ACA.

Power and Responsibility: Ethics on the Job

By Lt. Col. Willard M. Stovall

You must remember that you are a professional in an occupation that maintains high standards. Ethical behavior, along with professionalism, has to be the cornerstone of the daily execution of your duties.

As a correctional officer, you must hold yourself to a higher ethical standard than the inmates in your charge hold themselves. Many inmates will not hesitate to lie to you if it fits their purpose, but your own conduct is bound by high moral and ethical standards.

You have control over people who have at some point in their lives lost control, resulting in their incarceration. As a correctional officer, you have a lot of power over inmates; power that must be tempered with ethical conduct on your part. Your work places you well above those over whom you have power.

As the deputy commandant at the U.S. Disciplinary Barracks (USDB) in Fort Leavenworth, Kansas, I have a wide range of powers. I am second in charge of the Department of Defense's only maximum security prison, and I can make life pretty uncomfortable for any inmate who crosses me. The inmates are aware of this and will tell me, "Yo, Sir, you the Man."

Every now and then I run across an inmate who wants to see if he can put one over on me and get me to do something that will benefit him. Inmate "Smith" was nearly successful in doing just that.

Lt. Col. Willard M. Stovall is deputy commandant at the U.S. Disciplinary Barracks in Fort Leavenworth, Kansas.

One Friday, Smith told me that his lawyer had just called him and told him that his sentence had been cut to twenty months. Smith stated that he needed to be released right away because he had been at the USDB for two years. I immediately sprang into action. Overtime was authorized. I didn't care how they did it, I wanted Smith released before the end of the duty day. I was fired up over the injustice of holding a man beyond his sentence . . . until a division chief came to my office and told me that Smith had served only sixteen months and was not eligible for release, even with the reduced sentence.

Smith had taken advantage of my desire to be fair and made me look like a fool in front of my staff. I headed straight to Smith's cell and demanded to know why he told me he had been incarcerated for two years. He looked me straight in the eye and said, "Well, sir, it felt like I had been here for two years." He showed no remorse or discomfort for having lied to me. I was so angry, my first impulse was to make life totally miserable for Smith during the little time he had left at the USDB. But, even through my anger, I knew it would be ethically wrong to do so.

Correctional officers run into situations like this every day. Your ethical standards are tested constantly by inmates who hold you to a higher ethical standard than they hold themselves. It would be easy for you to "poke sticks in the cage" of an inmate who has just gotten on your "last good nerve," but you must not give in to those impulses. You must remember that you are a professional in an occupation that maintains high standards. Ethical behavior, along with professionalism, has to be the cornerstone of the daily execution of your duties. One of the key elements of ethical behavior is caring about what you do for a living.

Caring

Caring is closely associated with ethical behavior because when you have a personal stake in the successful accomplishment of your duties, you have high standards. It is frustrating and challenging to supervise violent and dysfunctional inmates on a daily basis; it's easy to turn off that part of you that cares about your fellow man. But in accepting the position of correctional officer, you must resist the urge to shut yourself off. You cannot do a good job if you do not care about what you do.

Being responsible and ethical often takes a lot of work. Inmate Brown was a correctional officer's nightmare. He was assaultive, foul-mouthed, and stubborn. He had one quality correctional officers assigned to his unit liked: when he told you he was going to do something, you could depend on him to do it. If he said that he was going to behave, you would have no problem with him. If Brown told correctional officers, "I'm going to stop acting up at noon tomorrow," at noon the next day, all problems with Brown would cease. On the other hand, when he told officers, "I'm going to get one of you," the Special Operations Reaction Team (SORT) was put on standby status. Brown hoped that being disruptive at the USDB would lead to a transfer to the Federal Bureau of Prisons (BOP). He thought that if he were transferred to BOP, he would be released sooner. After several years of using SORT to handle Brown's disruptive behavior, we decided to use a different approach on Brown. Discipline was still appropriate, but we needed to let him know that the institution itself cared about what happened to him. The institution had been exercising its power over Brown, but had not expressed its ethical responsibility to foster behavioral changes in him.

The institution's goal was to encourage Brown to adopt appropriate behavior. To do that we had to find out how we could get through to him. We had to discover his soft spot or what he cared about. This effort involved all staff who came into contact with Brown. Mental health staff made sure the chaplains knew what was going on. Security staff made sure they communicated with each other as to Brown's moods on any particular day so that everyone knew what to expect. We searched for his "on button" until one day we found it: his mother. Brown let his guard down one day and mentioned to an officer that his mother was very important to him.

We called her and asked for her help in our effort to correct Brown's behavior. She was skeptical but agreed to work with us. She agreed to visit her son. We told Brown that he would be allowed to visit with his mother if he consistently displayed appropriate behavior. He agreed. Soon after the visit with his mother, Brown told the officer on duty that he was tired of acting like a kid: "I give up. You win." No matter how long you've been a correctional officer, you feel good when you get that one problem inmate to agree to try to clean up his act.

We had the power to punish Brown every time he broke the rules, and we had the responsibility to make him abide by the rules. But we also had an ethical responsibility to get him to internalize his need to abide by the rules so that he could successfully reach his release date. One of the key missions of corrections is to get the inmate personally involved in his or her own rehabilitation.

Maintaining Standards

In his speech at the American Correctional Association's 1991 Congress, Frank Wood, former warden of the Minnesota Correctional Facility in Stillwater said: "Inmates are people who have made mistakes, but they are not mistakes." I had the opportunity to see this philosophy at work when I toured the Minnesota facility. While I was on tour, I noticed inmates and correctional officers treating each other with mutual respect. Of course, rules and procedures had to be followed, but officers at the Minnesota facility showed that this could be done and discipline maintained while treating inmates with respect and expecting them to behave appropriately.

Ethics is an integral part of our business. Inmates hold us to that higher standard than they hold themselves because we have not done anything wrong that caused us to be employed at a penal institution. We *chose* this as our profession and, therefore, have to abide by the rules of the profession.

Webster's Dictionary defines ethical behavior as behavior that conforms to the standards of conduct of a given profession or group. One of the American Correctional Association's ongoing efforts is to "develop and promote effective standards for the care, custody, training and treatment of offenders in all age groups and all areas of the correctional field" as well as "to promote the professional development of correctional staff at all levels." These are our professional guidelines. These are the rules by which we work and conduct ourselves.

Correctional officers practice these ethical rules daily as they interact with inmates and other correctional professionals. Every day can present challenges. In one case, a newly hired correctional officer was allowing himself to be personally involved with the inmates in his charge. Officer "Jones" was the same age as the inmates he supervised and felt more comfortable interacting with the inmates than with other staff. His supervisors could have allowed him to continue this pattern until Jones had done enough for them to fire him, but a better, more professional and ethical approach was to confront him, admonish him, and move him to another section of the institution where he could receive intense one-on-one mentoring by a supervisor. The end result? Jones was "salvaged" rather than fired. The institution had the power to get rid of Jones, but more important, it had the ethical responsibility to work with him to correct (rather than penalize) his performance of his duties. The end product was a correctional officer who was able to capably interact with inmates and who knew, firsthand, why he had to conduct himself according to established rules.

An institution's rules provide you with a road map that works for you as well as the inmates you control daily. Correctional officers who are open to bribery from an inmate (or the family of an inmate) will lose effectiveness.

Inmate "Doe" professed to be in love with the officer who supervised him. When he was allowed to go home for a temporary home parole visit, his family bought another ticket for the officer, who accompanied him on the same plane. Somebody turned them in and they were caught as they deplaned together. The officer was fired. Doe appealed his disciplinary action by stating that he should not be punished severely because, after all, he was a man and had certain "urges" that are exacerbated by incarceration. He was particularly upset because his custody status was reduced and other than this *small incident,* "I've been a model inmate."

What are the ethical implications of this incident? The correctional officer lost her job. She did not follow the rules, and she violated the ethical standards of her profession. The inmate lost a custody grade and some good conduct time, but gained an inmate war story that will last him a long time.

Treating inmates with respect and being ethical and fair in your interactions with them benefit both you and the inmates. Beginning on 11 May 1992, the USDB had a major inmate disturbance, the first of its kind in our facility in decades. Over a two-day period, 900 inmates in various stages of disobedience refused to lock down. We had instances of inmates controlling areas in which correctional officers were isolated. In every case, one of the following happened: (1) the correctional officers were allowed to remain and were not harassed, (2) if someone threatened a correctional officer, an inmate would step in and actually state, "You'll have to go through me first," or (3) the inmates would make a very clear and distinct action of raising their hands to shoulder height, stepping back, and telling supervisory personnel who had come to get the correctional officer to take him out of the area and that nobody was going to harm him.

Not a single correctional officer was harmed or held hostage. Would this happen in every correctional facility? Of course not, but it does happen in some. If *you* were the correctional officer surrounded by a group of hostile inmates who you normally supervise, how would they treat you? I'm not saying that you should behave as though you are competing in a popularity contest. You should perform your correctional duties with an even-handed, consistently ethical tone that demands respect from inmates because you daily demonstrate that you have proper standards.

Conclusion

Corrections is a dynamic and growing field. As a correctional officer, you are faced with many challenges and with the opportunities to make important contributions to society. We need correctional officers who will work ethically with the growing number of our fellow citizens who are incarcerated. As a correctional officer, you should exercise your power and responsibility ethically and return as many offenders as possible to society as productive citizens.

Moving Ahead in Your Career

By Harry K. Singletary, Jr.

> *Success is to be measured not so much by the position that one has reached in life, as by the obstacles which he has overcome while trying to succeed.*
>
> *Booker T. Washington*

I am a twenty-four-year veteran of corrections and the head of the fourth largest correctional system in the country. My appointment to secretary of corrections for the State of Florida is not the result of luck, wealth, or political influence; my position was earned by working, growing, and learning a little bit at a time each day over the past twenty-four years.

Corrections is not a lazy person's profession. Those who choose this profession must be aware of and understand the trends in corrections. They must constantly work at learning more about the profession.

Before embarking on a career in corrections, one must realize that corrections is a serious business. Those in corrections are responsible for administering sanctions imposed on individuals by the courts. They are dedicated to carrying out that mission by maintaining a safe, just, and humane environment in correctional institutions and facilities. Protecting the public, staff, inmates, and public property is their first, and most important, responsibility.

Corrections is constantly changing, with the work environment growing increasingly complex and dangerous. Crowding has placed a high degree of stress on the system, staff, and inmates.

Harry K. Singletary, Jr., is secretary of the Florida Department of Corrections.

The inmate profile has changed, with more inmates serving longer sentences for violent crimes than ever before. The system is receiving individuals who historically would have been held in mental health facilities if it were not for deinstitutionalization. The correctional environment is unpredictable, dangerous, and volatile.

Several demographic factors are altering the workplace and creating new challenges for present and future correctional professionals. By the year 2000, the work force will be more diverse with an increased percentage of women, older workers, and racial minorities. Minority groups, in terms of staff as well as inmates, will play critical roles that will affect the correctional agenda.

Establishing a Goal

My career in corrections began at the Reception and Diagnostic Center in Joliet, Illinois, on 31 October 1968. I worked with juvenile offenders and was moved by what I saw, heard, and experienced. I was twenty-two years old—not much older than the juveniles I supervised—and I felt I could influence them in a positive way. I always wanted to make a difference in the lives of others and corrections seemed to present the opportunity to do so.

After working a couple of weeks at the center, I decided to make corrections my career. Two months later, I set my career goal—to one day be superintendent of corrections. I did some homework to find out what kinds of skills and background I would need to reach my goal. Then, I developed the following outline:

1. I determined just what it was that I would have to learn in my present position and began studying the agency's policies and procedures. I knew I had to be dedicated to working long and hard.

2. I developed a plan to acquire and sharpen the skills and abilities necessary to be an effective administrator.

3. I discussed my plans with my family and asked for their feedback and support.

4. I developed a program designed to complete my plan and made a commitment to attain my goal by any and all legitimate means necessary.

I thought my plan was complete until I met Samuel Sublett, Jr., who was then superintendent of the Illinois Youth Center at St. Charles. After working with Sublett, I decided to model my administrative style after his. He was my mentor—someone who would guide me through my career ups and downs, listen to me, tell me what I needed to know, not what I wanted to hear. Anyone starting a career in corrections should find a mentor. A mentor should be someone who is accessible and knowledgeable; someone you respect.

Attitude

A positive attitude can advance any career. Attitude is more important than past failures or accomplishments, education, skills, money, physical appearance, and any other mitigating circumstances. Attitude is more important than what other people think, say, or do. Your attitude will make or break your career.

An individual controls his or her attitude. A winning attitude can be the driving force for a successful career. Life's failures and successes are 10 percent the result of what happens to us and 90 percent what we do with what happens to us.

Career-moving Tips

The following are some key elements to moving ahead in a career in corrections:

1. Be in touch with your biases. Be ever mindful of your biases, experiences, perceptions, beliefs, and attitudes. Do not suppress or hide them, rather, use them to examine your decisions—to be certain your actions are constitutionally right rather than personally motivated. If an individual has a problem with someone because of his or her age, sex, religious beliefs, or ethnicity, the individual should keep that perception always before him or her. Doing so ensures he or she will treat that person fairly and according to the principles of the profession and not according to his or her personal biases.

    Correctional professionals need to be a part of the solution. They should promote fairness as they carry out their daily duties. By example corrections professionals can teach respect for the law.

2. Know who you are and where you are going. Have an accurate self-perception. Make an honest assessment of your strengths and weaknesses. Accept responsibility and act responsibly. Learn from your mistakes and do not blame others or circumstances. Understand your circumstances, set priorities, chart a course, make adjustments, and push ahead to accomplish your tasks.

   Maintain self-control and be self-reliant, using tenacity and stamina to persevere. Believe in yourself and your abilities.

3. Keep an open mind. Be open to new ideas and new ways to complete tasks. Don't get stuck in the past—it prevents one from thinking, dreaming, and creating a vision for the future. Be eager to develop new approaches and insights, occasionally reviewing old decisions to ensure they are still viable and applicable to present conditions.

   Develop an internal and external environment that encourages creativity. Don't be afraid to fail—failure is not the end, but a new beginning at problem solving.

4. Have a sense of humor. Corrections professionals should take their work and responsibilities seriously, but they should also try to see the humor in life.

5. Have a sense of perspective. Nothing is as bad as it first seems. Get all the facts and consider all options before becoming too anxious and jumping to conclusions.

6. Have a sense of compassion. Take time to consider the feelings of others. Treat people fairly.

7. Maintain integrity. Stand up for your convictions. Take responsibility for your actions and share the credit with everyone involved. On the other hand, if something goes wrong, accept responsibility and move on.

8. Maintain credibility. Be reliable and consistent. Be honest and tell the truth even when it hurts.

A Career-moving Attitude

Supervisors perceive their most essential subordinates to be those with a career-moving attitude. These individuals are recognized, trained, and encouraged to participate in the agency. They are respected and valued as individuals who are well-versed in the department's mission and philosophy, versatile, and able to fill many roles.

What are the characteristics of individuals with career-moving attitudes? These individuals perform their daily tasks because of who they are, not because of who they work for or because someone is competing with them or looking over their shoulders. They act as professionals and are driven by internal principles, values, ethics, and a code of conduct that is above reproach. They are part of a team and work actively with supervisors to achieve mutually beneficial goals. They avoid unnecessary confrontation, but will always stand up for ideals and principles they believe are fair and vital to the agency's mission.

A career-moving attitude allows officers to become self-managers and self-starters who work equally as hard whether their supervisor is or is not looking. They have original ideas and produce answers as well as questions. They are honest with their supervisors and keep them informed.

Corrections is 5 percent hardware and 95 percent people. Moving ahead in your career means making something of yourself and taking others along with you. Try your best to get to the top, if that is where you want to be, but remember that the more people you take along with you, the faster you will get there and the longer you will stay.

Conclusion

You must be a friend to yourself, have respect for yourself, and be a success with yourself before you can succeed with others. A good attitude and a positive self-image are your greatest assets.

Wellness: An Important Lifestyle Choice for Correctional Officers

By Vicki D. Verdeyen, Ed.D.

The concepts of physical and psychological well-being are especially important for correctional officers because they work in stressful environments.

I remember as a child hearing my father say, "If you have your health, you have everything." My appreciation for the meaning of this conventional wisdom has increased as I have grown older. Physical well-being is a necessary state for productivity at work and for enjoyment of leisure activities while not at work. Psychological well-being is necessary for accurately processing interactions with others and the environment so that an individual can respond with the appropriate emotions, learn from experiences, and grow in wisdom.

What Is Wellness?

The term "wellness" was coined in 1961 by H. Dunn in his book, *High Level Wellness.* Dunn highlighted the process of each person attending to his or her health. He explained that wellness was synonymous with excellent health and led to "an improved quality of life, human excellence, and high energy" (Ivancevich 1988).

Vicki D. Verdeyen, Ed.D., is the regional psychology administrator for the Mid-Atlantic Region of the Federal Bureau of Prisons.

The opinions expressed in this article are not necessarily those of the Federal Bureau of Prisons or of the U.S. Department of Justice.

In the correctional setting, wellness deals with health promotion and the prevention of psychological and physiological problems in correctional workers. Wellness means having a healthy life style: being physically fit; undergoing routine health screening; eating nutritious foods and maintaining a balanced diet; managing stress; and avoiding substance abuse, such as smoking, drinking alcohol, and using drugs.

The Importance of Wellness for Correctional Officers

The concepts of physical and psychological well-being are especially important for correctional officers because they work in stressful environments. Some of the stressors associated with corrections include inherent stressors, such as threat to life and safety and hostile interactions with inmates; administrative stressors, such as poor equipment, crowded conditions, and an overload of paperwork; and societal stressors, such as lack of public support and close scrutiny of behavior by courts or politicians (Norvell 1990).

Additionally, corrections is physically demanding work because emergency situations are mixed unpredictably with routine, tedious activities. An emergency situation requiring an officer to run, restrain an inmate, and move him or her to a cell places an exceptional demand on the mental and physical state of the officer. After an incident like this, the officer usually returns to routine activities, such as doing paperwork, serving meals, or conducting counts. It is this mixture of activities that produces more physical and psychological stress than either sustained emergency work (such as working in a hospital emergency room) or sustained routine work (such as filing or assembly line work).

Hostage situations, riots, homicides, and suicides are examples of incidents that produce extremely high levels of stress for correctional employees. As described in *Employee Assistance: Professional Report*, "the already high level of stress which law enforcement professionals experience is exacerbated by the subculture's values of the superman [superwoman] complex." In other words, there is an expectation or demand that correctional workers should not show weakness or appear to be out of control. Additionally, having problems is sometimes considered to be a sign of weakness. For these reasons, correctional workers often deny their stress and neglect their mental health needs (Employee Assistance Report 1992).

Agency-sponsored Wellness Programs

Situations requiring exceptional physical and emotional responses are common in the corrections environment. It certainly makes good sense then for correctional officers to prepare themselves for this through involvement in wellness programs.

Many correctional agencies offer employee assistance programs. Through these programs, officers can receive counseling, support, or referral to other professional agencies.

Officers should turn to agency-sponsored wellness programs to help them deal with work place trauma, such as hostage situations, riots, or other stressful incidents. Officers who know that being involved in such situations can lead to difficulty sleeping, nightmares, stomach problems, irritability, and depression can prepare themselves for these symptoms. Knowing that these effects are normal physical and psychological consequences of trauma that often dissipate after a few weeks can be reassuring. If these symptoms do not go away, or if they intensify, officers should seek a support system, such as counseling.

Elements to Developing Individual Programs

Officers should develop their own wellness programs. An effective program can be broken down into key elements: evaluation, education, exercise, and commitment.

Evaluation

Evaluation includes an assessment of individual needs and resources. Correctional officers should evaluate their physical and psychological strengths and weaknesses through self-assessment or evaluation by their medical doctor, trainer, or health specialist. Effective wellness programs begin with accurate and comprehensive evaluation. Officers who have recently undergone physical examinations and whose physicians have recommended exercise programs without limitations are well on their way to developing an effective wellness program. On the other hand, if officers have high blood pressure or other significant health concerns, then further professional evaluation and discussion is warranted.

Education

Education is another element of an effective program. "Educational approaches are the treatment of choice when the objective of a health promotion program is to increase awareness and knowledge regarding health risks and health-enhancing alternatives" (Frautschi 1987). Today self-education is easier than ever. Correctional officers may simply begin to pay more attention to health-related information on television and in magazines and books. Topics range from information on toxins in the environment, to chemicals used in food preparation, to the benefits of walking versus running.

Exercise

No wellness program would be complete without exercise. Because exercise often evokes visions of sweat and tears, this element may be the most difficult to implement. For this reason, participants must ask themselves a key question: "Which activity will most likely sustain my interest?"

Most experts agree that doing anything in terms of exercise— whether it be bicycling, running, aerobic dancing, or walking—is better than doing nothing. Correctional officers assigned to a housing unit might try wearing a pedometer at work to determine how many miles they actually walk in a day. Officers who discover that they walk a great deal on the job may want to select an exercise activity that is different from walking, such as lifting weights to develop upper-body muscles.

Commitment

Commitment is the final element critical to an officer's wellness program. Getting started can be difficult, but the real challenge is staying with the program. There is more than one method of staying committed, and again it is important for individuals to find what works for him or her. I have a friend who has worked in corrections for almost twenty years; he began running about five years ago. I asked him one day how he stayed so committed to his running, since he rarely misses a day. He said he decided that he needed to run for health reasons and knew it simply had to be done. On the other hand, I know people who have stayed committed to their wellness programs because they have made them fun, by listening to their favorite music or walking with companions. Once again, if individuals accurately and realistically evaluate themselves, they will be able to determine what will work best for them as they design their wellness lifestyle.

Conclusion

Ultimately, a successful wellness program is the responsibility of the individual. "The person is given primary responsibility for his or her achievement of health" (Ivancevich 1988). However, correctional officers should also look to programs that may be offered by their correctional agencies as wellness resources. Maintaining a healthy lifestyle is important on the job as well as off. Healthy correctional officers are generally more alert on the job, which reduces accidents and enhances safety for staff and inmates. These officers are also able to enjoy leisure activities with family and friends.

References

Stevens Publishing. February 1992. *Employee Assistance Professional Report* 2 (1).

Frautschi, N. M., and G. E. Swan. 1987. Health promotion in the workplace: Guidelines for the clinical evaluator. In *Applications in behavioral medicine and health psychology: A clinician's source book*, J. A. Blumentahl and D. C. McKee eds. Sarasota, Fl.: Professional Resource Exchange.

Ivancevich, J. M., and M. T. Matteson. 1988. Promoting the individual's health and well-being. In *Causes, coping, and consequences of stress at work*, C. L. Cooper and R. Payne eds. New York: John Wiley & Sons.

Norvell, N., and D. Belles. 1990. *Stress management training: A group leader's guide*. Sarasota, Fl.: Professional Resource Exchange.

Staff Substance Abuse

By Lanson Newsome

Substance abuse will always be a serious problem, particularly in a correctional setting. Correctional officers who are substance abusers must seek help.

A few years ago two transfer officers from Georgia State Prison, a maximum security facility, were transporting an inmate from the facility to a medical treatment prison about 200 miles away. En route, the inmate freed himself from his restraints with a handcuff key he had concealed, drew a small caliber, derringer-type weapon, and pointed it at the head of one of the officers. The inmate told the officers that he was commandeering the vehicle and if they did not follow his instructions he would kill them. Knowing the inmate had a history of escapes, with one involving gunfire, the officers went along with his demands. After ordering them to throw their weapons out of the vehicle, the inmate instructed them to turn onto a narrow side road. In an uninhabited area, he ordered them to stop the vehicle and get out. The inmate then handcuffed the officers and made his escape on foot.

When the vehicle did not arrive at the medical institution and the officers did not respond to repeated radio calls, a statewide alert was posted and a search initiated. The officers were found a few hours later, and the inmate was captured in an adjoining state the same day. The inmate claimed that an officer working at the prison had given him the weapon, ammunition, and handcuff key.

The accused officer admitted he had brought the inmate a weapon and many other items, including drugs, over the past

Lanson Newsome is deputy commissioner of the Georgia Department of Corrections.

months. He said he smuggled the contraband to the inmate in exchange for money to support his own drug habit.

Employees new to corrections work may wonder how this could happen. Knowing the danger a firearm in a prison can present to staff and inmates, not to mention the risk of prosecution if discovered, how could a correctional officer do something like this?

Correctional officers who have worked around inmates for any length of time, especially in maximum security prisons, know how this can happen. They also know it will probably happen again. In this case, the officer thought he had found an easy way to relieve the stress he experienced on the job—by taking drugs. In addition, he got caught up in one of the oldest and most dangerous con games inmates play on staff.

Correctional officers who drink excessively or abuse drugs are especially susceptible to inmate manipulation. Some inmates are skilled at understanding and reading behavior. They look for a "weakness" they can exploit. Whether it's compassion, fear, or perhaps an unfulfilled need, these inmates know what to look for and how to manipulate it. By the time the officer realizes what is going on—if ever—it's usually too late to stop.

In prison it's known as a setup. In their book *Games Criminals Play*, Allen and Bosta (1981) state: "Whether staff like it or not, the critical eye of the inmate is a twenty-four hour companion. . . . The [setup] process is subtle, the victim unsuspecting; it is covert, but undetected until the damage is done. . . ." That's what happened to the officer in this situation. Even if the officer had refused to supply the inmate with a handgun and instead confessed to the warden that he had been bringing prohibited items into the prison, he probably would have been prosecuted.

What factors contributed to this situation? The officer admitted to using marijuana and alcohol to relieve stress he experienced on the job. The inmate worked to gain the officer's confidence and initiated conversations with the officer. One thing they discussed was the officer's use of marijuana and alcohol. Once he had this information, the inmate knew he had the officer hooked.

Stress on the Job

A substance abuser is not necessarily a crackhead hanging out at a crack house or a wino passed out in an alley. Substance abuse, particularly alcohol abuse, is a fact of life for many average citizens who have families and hold down jobs. In fact, the National Institute on Drug Abuse (1991) reports that 51 percent of the U.S. population abuses alcohol.

Many factors contribute to substance abuse. One factor is the degree of stress in a person's life.

Working in a prison is one of the most stressful jobs you will find. Think about the psychological environment of a prison. Your job consists of keeping inmates confined in a place they don't want to be. You are constantly exerting your authority over inmates to ensure order is maintained. There is an ongoing "battle of wits" between inmates and staff. Inmates are usually trying to gain something—extra recreation time, extra personal items, contraband—which means they are probably going against your authority. In addition, inmates are usually competing among themselves for something of value or to gain a degree of control. Correctional officers have to be aware of their surroundings constantly, maintaining a never-ending vigil to ensure inmates don't get out of line. All this creates a high degree of stress.

Then there is the physical environment. Imagine the intensity of a multitiered, maximum security cellblock housing two or three hundred inmates: the constant noise level, the jumble of sounds, the frantic activity. Add to that crowding, where, in some cases, two inmates are assigned to a cell designed for one. There's the constant threat of violence against an inmate or an officer.

There are demands made on correctional staff by their peers and supervisors. Supervisors may place difficult demands on officers, who may then view supervisors as insensitive and uncaring. Or for various reasons, there may be a shortage of staff, which forces officers to work longer hours than usual.

Other demands are self-imposed. Correctional officers do not want to appear weak or frightened in front of inmates or each other; therefore, they may act in a way that would normally be out of character outside the institution. All of these situations create stress.

The officer who brought contraband into prison was a relatively new employee who was assigned to work in a maximum security cellblock. He was in constant contact with some of the most hardened, devious, and violent criminals found in a correctional system. Working a cellblock range alone for most the day, his interactions were not with other officers but with inmates. Because he lacked authority over the inmates, he attempted to maintain control by persuasion and suggestion. When the inmates learned he could be manipulated, what little control the officer had was lost.

This officer turned to marijuana and alcohol to cope with the situation. He is not the first nor will he be the last to do so. As one officer said in *Prison Officers and Their World* (Kauffman 1988), "I was drinking to get up enough nerve to go [in] and when I got out of work I'd get loaded just to forget. . . . I'd go out at night and sometimes not come home, just stay out and get loaded all night long because I didn't want to think about going to work the next day." This is not unusual behavior for someone unable to adequately cope with the demands of prison work.

Drug Testing

In 1984, the Georgia Department of Corrections initiated a program for testing inmates for marijuana and cocaine use (see Table 1). In January 1985, all job applicants were being tested. Staff testing followed in July. The majority of staff was receptive to this idea. They were aware of the kinds of problems drugs can cause in a prison and realized that drug testing is in the best interest of staff and inmates.

Substance abusers who might have applied for a job with the Department in the past realized that doing so now, with mandatory drug testing, would be a waste of time. More employees asked for help to overcome drug dependency, and fewer inmates were found using drugs. It is likely that there is a direct correlation between the two.

TABLE 1

Results of Drug Tests for the Georgia Department Of
Corrections, 1984-1989

Year	# Tested	# Tested Positive	% Tested Positive
Inmates			
1984	492	41	8.3
1985	412	30	7.3
1986	725	25	3.4
1987	692	10	1.4
1988	695	11	1.6
1989	626	14	2.2
Applicants			
1985	224	25	11.2
1986	184	8	4.3
1987	241	6	2.5
1988	208	2	1.0
1989	304	2	0.66
Staff			
1985 (July)	328	5	1.5
1986	759	11	1.4
1987	760	5	0.66
1988	766	1	0.13
1989	724	3	0.41

Drug testing sends a signal to both staff and inmates that drugs have no place in a prison. Correctional officers who abuse drugs face a greater risk than ever of losing their jobs. Officers who don't abuse drugs can feel reassured that fellow officers are drug-free and therefore dependable.

Help for Substance Abusers

Correctional officers who are substance abusers must seek help. Help is available in many forms: private counseling; community groups, such as Alcoholics Anonymous and Narcotics Anonymous; and counseling programs offered by the agency.

Officers with substance abuse problems should realize that their agency is concerned about keeping good employees and maintaining safety for staff, inmates, and the public. Programs agencies provide to help their officers overcome substance abuse problems are in place to help, not to single out, employees with problems.

One example is the employee assistance program developed by the Georgia State Prison to help employees with alcohol abuse problems. The program began as an in-house referral program with existing staff, medical doctors, clinical chaplains, psychiatrists, and psychologists who worked with staff who asked for help. An employee who was a recovering alcoholic helped to direct the effort.

In addition to seeking professional help, employees with substance abuse problem should try to help themselves by developing self-esteem and a positive self-image. Environment affects behavior and attitudes. Correctional officers should always remember that they are professionals. Professional appearance and demeanor improve attitudes. If officers act professionally in their interactions with inmates, inmates will have more respect for them. Ultimately, this should reduce the job's stress level.

It is also important for staff who do not abuse drugs or alcohol to be aware of the problems associated with substance abuse. A fellow officer's substance abuse problem may very well become their problem if that officer can not be relied on to carry out his or her duties. Officers rely on each other for safety.

Conclusion

Substance abuse will always be a serious problem, particularly in a correctional setting. Correctional officers who are substance abusers must seek help. They should participate in programs offered by their agencies and communities to get help. Correctional officers with substance abuse problems endanger other staff, inmates, the public, and themselves.

References

Allen, B., and D. Bosta. 1981. *Games criminals play: How you can profit by knowing them.* Susanville, Calif.: Rae John Publishers.

National Institute on Drug Abuse. 1991. *Summary of findings from the 1991 household survey on drug abuse.* Rockville, Md.: National Institute on Drug Abuse.

Kauffman, K. 1988. *Prison officers and their world.* Cambridge, Mass.: Harvard University Press.

Correctional Officers and Their Families: Dealing with Stress

By Fred Van Fleet, Ph.D.

A positive attitude about yourself and your career in corrections is one of the most effective inoculations against stress that threatens you and your family.

A correctional officer and his wife came to me because of problems with their marriage. Even in a psychologist's office, the correctional officer had difficulty showing his true feelings. He tried to make light of his wife's many complaints and even joked that she could not possibly be serious about not loving him. At this point, his wife looked him squarely in the eye and stated: "I lie awake some nights thinking of ways to kill you."

This was his second marriage. I wondered whether his first wife had the same antipathy as the second. Had the officer learned anything from these relationships? Had he learned to consider the needs of others? Had he acquired a sense of responsibility toward them? Apparently not, for when I encountered him about a year later, he was with his new fiancee, had been drinking, was in a wildly expansive mood, and demonstrated the same shallowness and lack of insight as before. His colleagues saw him as a "great guy." He was a respected correctional officer. I saw him as a walking time bomb, and I felt sorry for his new fiancee, who seemed to be falling into his trap. Fortunately for her, she broke off their engagement. Shortly thereafter, the officer killed himself.

Fred Van Fleet, Ph.D., is a forensic psychologist and a consultant on issues in corrections.

The husband of one correctional officer complained that his wife's negativity and foul language not only distressed him and his children, but made it practically impossible for them to socialize outside of correctional circles. He was embarrassed by his wife and felt estranged from her. She, in turn, could no longer relate to outsiders and only felt comfortable socializing with other correctional officers.

Unfortunately, these examples of problems correctional officers and their families face are not unusual. There are many similar cases being documented every day. Is there something about a career in corrections that threatens family stability?

Many sources of stress have been identified in correctional work. Besides obvious stressors like shift work and the threat of danger, there are more subtle factors, such as negative public image, poor morale, and a sense of ambiguity about the correctional officer's role, that may result in generalized states of anxiety or tension that may be taken home to the family. These factors contribute to either cumulative stress (an overload phenomenon) or traumatic stress (which often results in acute, intense anxieties). In either case, the family should not be allowed to fall victim to stress; the family should be considered part of the antidote to stress.

Although families should be important therapeutic assets, they are often, in fact, liabilities. In many cases, when the officer faces excessive levels of work-related pressure, his or her family members are unable and even, in a few cases, unwilling to participate in the prescribed treatment. They are unable to provide empathy and support because, for too many years, they have been shut out. Family members often tell me, "Whenever I try to get him to open up, he just glares at me" or "Whenever I reach out to him, he pulls away." For a long time I believed it was only the families of male officers who felt that way, but years of experience proved that this was a phenomenon common to all correctional officers, both male and female.

Male correctional officers feel the need to continuously project a tough male image, especially outside the work place. They forget that family members respond best to love, tenderness, and sensitivity, not to power. Female officers must resist the urge to adopt masculine traits so that they can fit in and be "one of the boys." Adopting macho attitudes can have devastating effects on their home life.

Yes, there are aspects of correctional work that may threaten family stability, but there are also ways of coping with these factors.

Dealing with Stress

Although many different techniques are used to handle stress, many involve three common elements: focus, attitude, and communication.

Focus

It is important to be as dedicated to your family as you are to your career. Keep your priorities in focus—long after you retire, you will want your family by your side. Many individuals approaching their later years long for another chance to do right by their families. For many, it is too late. You should fit your career into your family; don't try to fit your family into your career.

Sometimes the best way to cope with work-related stress is through the help of family members. Correctional officers often mask their feelings while they are on the job, but find it difficult to keep up the act when at home. In one family counseling session, a woman tried to outline for her husband all the signs he was giving that things weren't quite right. Each time she mentioned something, he became defensive and dismissed her concerns as irrelevant or unimportant. Finally, in exasperation, their twelve-year-old son, who had been sitting quietly for most of the session, blurted out, "Dad, you're not coping, and we all know it." The correctional officer finally began to realize that he was indeed suffering from stress. Accepting that he had a problem made him open to treatment.

When faced with cumulative stressors (too much on your plate or stress building up over time), it is often necessary to recognize your abilities and limitations so that you can find a realistic way to lighten the load. Professional burnout is often the result of not effectively dealing with cumulative stress.

39

Burnout often is experienced by fine employees who just don't know how to say, "Enough is enough."

If you feel overwhelmed by stress, don't be afraid to ask your family physician or a psychologist for help. Their feedback often carries a lot of weight with employers, without prejudice. You are a valued employee, and the system does not want to lose your services. It makes more sense for your organization to work with you rather than to hire and train someone else.

Correctional officers are always faced with the threat of being involved in a crisis situation. If the problems facing you and your family are the result of trauma or a critical incident, you and your family should seek professional help immediately. Individuals suffering post-traumatic disorders respond well to therapy and counseling, and many problems can be prevented through early intervention.

Many correctional organizations offer employee/family assistance programs, debriefing sessions, and peer-related support services. You and your family should use these services. Do not try to resolve potentially disastrous stress-effects by yourself, and do not ignore their warning signs. You may not even be aware of the signs of stress you are displaying. Listen to family members and learn from their feedback. Learn how to express yourself and make an effort to unwind at home.

Attitude

A positive attitude about yourself and your career in corrections is one of the most effective inoculations against stress that threatens you and your family. Your attitude shapes not only your self-image, but also the image you project to the public. Over the years, many husbands and wives of correctional officers have complained to me that they lie when asked what their spouses do for a living—not because they are ashamed of their spouses' work, but because their spouses are ashamed of working in corrections.

When entering this line of work, every officer must ask himself or herself whether this is just a job or is it a career in which he or she can take pride. If you can find no sense of job fulfillment and satisfaction, you should not work in corrections. Find some other employment more suitable to your needs. It will be healthier for both you and your family.

Officers may develop a negative self-image for a variety of reasons. A negative image of corrections is regularly portrayed in the media. Movies often portray officers as stupid, animalistic, and senseless abusers of socially wronged individuals who have somehow, mistakenly, become caught up in the brutal world of crime and criminals. The warden is often the worst abuser, and the most dangerous inmate is frequently the most sympathetic character.

This negative picture and false perception of reality cannot be changed by living up to that very image or by being ashamed of your chosen profession. In one maximum security facility, following every shift change, the correctional officers go to a local bar to unwind. Most are still in uniform, and many stay for hours and become raucous. This image is not lost on the members of the small community where the prison is located.

Few members of the general public have ever set foot inside a correctional facility or ever plan to. They witness crime through the daily news. The quieter things are, the happier they seem to be. Most become aware of corrections only when a facility is proposed in their community or when there is a disturbance, riot, or escape. Then they are likely to respond with hostility, and that hostility is generally misdirected at corrections. Changing the public's perception, and the media's portrayals may be difficult, but you can do your part by changing your own self-image and attitude.

In addition to dealing with the public's image of them, correctional officers need to deal with the inmates' perceptions of them. I once overheard an inmate say, "There is no excuse for welfare; anyone can get a job as a screw." His negative perception of correctional officers is probably based on his experiences with them.

Another inmate complimented a particular correctional officer by saying that he was "okay." That same inmate saved the lives of two correctional officers during a major inmate uprising because they had treated him fairly in the past.

Many correctional officers who have had their lives threatened on the job credit their survival to their professionalism. Many said that they treat inmates fairly and see them as human beings in need.

Corrections, like any other system, is imperfect, but it does offer rewards. Whether you are a burnout or a standout depends on you—your commitment and your attitude. Positive attitudes generate positive results. Your public image is a projection of your self-image.

Communication

Can you imagine the hazards of correctional work without proper communication? If you didn't have guidelines when you began your career, how would you know the proper interaction between a correctional officer and an inmate? Imagine being cut off from co-workers during an uprising, with no means to communicate. (Often, the absence of a radio can be a significant stressor.)

Yet, many who rely on basic communication during their every working hour, never consider that the same needs may exist at home. Whatever stressors you experience, your family experiences, albeit vicariously.

Keep your family informed about what is going on in your job—the challenges, frustrations, and goals. The more you communicate, the less uncertainty and apprehension there will be. If you are unsure how much you should share with your family—confidential information should be kept to yourself— let them know there are some things you cannot share with them.

Hold regular, but informal, debriefing sessions with family members who are old enough to participate. Discuss the highlights of your week, express some of your concerns, and share your feelings. You should listen to your family's feedback and answer their questions. Open and honest communication prevents needless anxiety and helps to keep you close to those you need and love.

Communicating with your family may not be easy, especially if you do not have appropriate communication skills. Some individuals may want their homes to be sanctuaries.

They avoid discussing any aspects of the job at home. Family members cannot be empathic or understanding if the individual does not open up to them.

At the other extreme is the individual who comes home and unloads all of the miseries of the day, every day, on his or her family. The individual may be unburdening himself or herself, but the burden is transferred to the family.

It is important to learn how much you need to share with your family, so as to raise awareness without raising anxiety. Problems you encounter on the job cannot always be left at the facility. The continuous adrenal flow associated with maximum security or a death row watch, an inmate suicide or homicide, the anticipation of a disturbance, a threat, or an assault on a fellow officer can lead to emotional arousal that stays with you long after the shift has ended. You may return home with feelings of frustration, fear, or anger that are difficult to share with those who have not experienced them directly.

Feelings should be articulated and expressed. Sometimes you may need time by yourself at the end of a shift; at other times you may need a shoulder to lean on or a sympathetic ear. Whatever the need, include family members in the process as much as possible.

You need to be sensitive to the stress experienced by family members as a result of your work. In one case, a correctional officer's wife went to pick up her husband after his shift. She was met at the front gate by an officer who told her that there was a hostage-taking in progress in the east wing. He said that one correctional officer had been killed and another was being held captive. Heavily armed police and emergency services vehicles were everywhere. The woman was concerned because her husband worked the east wing. She begged for more information, but none was forthcoming. She was advised to return home and wait. She was told that the warden would be in touch with her.

The woman went home and sat by her telephone waiting anxiously for prison officials to call with news about her husband. Several hours later, her husband arrived home safely. The warden never did call to apprise her of the situation. Her husband had not been in personal danger at any time; he was not in the area of the incident, nor was he directly involved in subsequent activities. His wife was a victim who had suffered extreme anxiety over her husband's safety.

Conclusion

Correctional work is one of the most stressful occupations in modern society. It is not without its rewards and challenges, but the pressures put on its employees and their families should not be ignored. Correctional officers serve a valuable social function, often without the recognition they deserve. As a correctional officer, you should interact with all segments of society and educate others about your profession.

Suggested Readings

Van Fleet, F. 1992. Debriefing and the critical incident. *EAP Digest* (March/April).

Van Fleet, F. 1991. Early intervention: Debriefing staff after disturbances can prevent years of pain. *Corrections Today* (July).

Correctional Officer Role Ambiguity

By Richard L. Stalder

As you train, work, and gain experience and exposure to the many facets of your job, there will be frequent opportunities to question how what you do under different circumstances or situations fits into any central theme or philosophy.

Your job as a correctional officer will often leave you scratching your head and wondering just how you fit into the system. As you enforce rules, resolve disputes, supervise housekeeping, distribute laundry, pass long nights in a guard tower, listen to complaints, announce counts, and spend hours hoping nothing happens and wishing something would to break the monotony, you will have cause to reflect on how you fit in.

The autonomy and simplicity of the traditional correctional model have been replaced by a complex and often conflicting network of rules and policies that is designed to satisfy the courts, advocacy groups, centralized administrative structures, and diverse regulatory agencies. A distinct shift in the judicial environment adds to the confusion. For the past several years, we in corrections have had to prove that our actions and policies had the least possible impact on the rights of inmates. We now defend what we do based on a test of reasonableness in relation to our "legitimate penological objectives" (*Turner v. Safley*, 107 S.Ct. 2254 [1978]).

Those of you who already have careers in corrections may have started out as "guards" and made midcareer shifts to a

Richard L. Stalder is secretary of the Louisiana Department of Public Safety and Corrections in Baton Rouge.

role more consistent with "counselor/helper." You will now find that "correctional officer" accurately describes your role. This marks a renewed focus on the primary goal of safety and the secondary goal of enabling change through the establishment of safe, organized, and disciplined correctional environments.

As you train, work, and gain experience and exposure to the many facets of your job, there will be frequent opportunities to question how what you do under different circumstances or situations fits into any central theme or philosophy. This chapter will first establish a broad and generally acceptable set of priorities and second, discuss duties that are a part of your job and those that are not.

Establishing Priorities

While volumes can and have been written outlining different theories about priorities during unusual or disturbance situations in the prison, there is little disagreement over what our priorities are in routine operations.

Ensuring Public Safety

It is the primary responsibility of each correctional officer to minimize the potential for escape, unauthorized absence, or other action by an inmate that could jeopardize public safety. The most sophisticated automated security systems and the hardest "jail house steel" serve only to complement a well-trained and qualified correctional officer.

Providing for the Safety of Staff and Inmates

The most significant factors contributing to the court's intervention in corrections in the past two decades have related to the ability of the institution to maintain a safe and stable internal environment. Your role as a correctional officer is of primary importance in achieving this goal. As you carry out your daily duties, the immediate safety and well-being of staff and inmates must be reflected in your performance. Is someone in your area of supervision being victimized? Does anything appear unusual or inconsistent with normal activities, noise levels, or the frequency of occurrence of minor incidents? Do you follow shakedown procedures thoroughly? Are you doing your part to keep weapons, drugs, and other dangerous items out of the prison?

While on the job, your safety depends on the people you work with and their motivation to function at the highest level possible consistent with their training and skills. Inmates must rely on your commitment to duty to protect them. Inmates' predatory, violent, and disruptive behavior will not be able to develop in an environment of reasonable discipline and organization. Correctional officers, in their everyday duties, must strive to establish and maintain this environment.

Providing and Maintaining an Appropriate Environment

Although it is important to keep the public safe and "keep the peace" inside, correctional officers in successful prisons have the responsibility to provide an opportunity for change in an environment of well-being.

Inmates have basic needs for medical and mental health care, adequate nutrition, and appropriate clothing and shelter. Providing them these services contributes to an environment of well-being. Correctional officers have the responsibility to upgrade the well-being of inmates who have identifiable deficiencies and then help them maintain a reasonable level of wellness.

In this environment of reasonable emphasis on security and safety and reasonable attention to basic human needs of inmates, it is important to provide resources that will enable inmates who are so motivated an opportunity for change. Without programs and services that enable constructive improvement in life skills, the chances of successful and lawful adjustment on release may be minimized. It is important to note that the individual needing change must seek help and work to take advantage of it. To effectively use limited resources for education and self-help programs, inmates motivated to change old patterns and acquire skills needed to adopt new, appropriate patterns should be encouraged to participate. It is also important to note that inmates will get maximum benefit from resources applied to enable change only when an organized and reasonably disciplined environment has been established.

Defining Your Role

It is difficult to define your specific role as a correctional officer because that definition depends on the role of your institution, the type and custody of inmates you work with, and your shift and assignment. It may be helpful to discuss what is *not* included in your role.

You Are Not a Doctor

It is 1:20 a.m. The same inmate who pesters you every evening with some small complaint or request presents himself at the officer's station and says his stomach hurts. You carefully assess his current physical condition—he walks, talks, and breathes—and decide there is no merit to his complaint. Then you reluctantly notify your supervisor, who ensures the inmate is seen by a qualified medical staff person who is responsible for medical examination and treatment.

This scene is common in large institutions. You may feel frustrated with a system that seems to provide a higher level of medical care than what you can afford for yourself and your family. You may wonder why so much time and money is spent on exaggerated complaints and nonexistent injuries and illnesses. You may be tempted to establish your own set of basic filters and screens—a triage system implemented at the correctional officer level.

In the end, however, you must realize that you are not trained or qualified to perform these functions. It should be a comfort to both you and the inmate that correctional facilities see to it that adequate medical delivery systems are now available on a twenty-four-hour basis to handle medical problems. It was not always this way. In the past, many correctional officers were forced to function in medical roles they were not qualified to handle, which resulted in inadequate care for inmates and in litigation against correctional officers and agencies. The only legitimate medical role you have is to administer first aid and/or cardiopulmonary resuscitation in emergency situations in accordance with your training.

You Are Not a Psychologist

Most inmates have difficulty adjusting to loss of freedom and separation from family and friends. Some cope with life in prison better than others. You will see inmates suffer loneliness and despair, and you may want to ease their suffering. Although your attentiveness to the needs of one person may go a long way toward easing his or her pain, there are people on the outside and other staff and inmates on the inside who rely on your attentiveness to the broad scope of your duties to ensure their safety and security. The issue of your role here is one of balance.

Helping inmates adjust to the reality of their current circumstances can contribute to the stability of the prison, but when interpersonal relationships and "helper" roles interfere with the performance of core custodial duties, they become inappropriate. The professional relationship of correctional officer to inmate differs from that of counselor to inmate. Correctional officers have a primary responsibility to the whole. Counselors have a primary responsibility to the individual. It is, however, a part of the correctional officer's job to be as alert to mental health emergencies as to medical emergencies. For example, the correctional officer is the most important link in the prevention of suicide through early detection of behavioral changes that may signal acute distress. The role of the officer is to identify and isolate problems so that intervention can then be accomplished by other staff.

You Are Not the Judge or the Jury

It may be difficult at times to put your personal feelings about an inmate's crime or background aside and deal with him or her objectively. You must remember that the sentence handed down by the court and the role of the prison itself in the criminal justice system constitute the elements of punishment, you do not. You should not second-guess the merit of a plea bargain or ponder the quirks of different sentences. You must be content to let each element of the system function in its own environment and dedicate yourself to the fair and professional performance of your duties.

You Take Abuse, You Cannot Give It

Perhaps the most frustrating aspect of the modern correctional officer's job is that the officer will be expected to take abuse, verbal or otherwise, and not be abusive in turn. The officer is not an instrument of immediate punishment for disruptive behavior. The correctional officer's role during confrontation is to defuse and control. It requires professionalism, training, and well-developed skills.

It is appropriate to acknowledge that tension and frustration exist. They develop in response to inmates striking out at correctional officers who represent a system that restricts their movements, activities, and pleasures. It is not appropriate to let that tension and frustration channel itself into outlets that are destructive or abusive. There is no larger or more important challenge than the development and consistent use of self-control, regardless of provocation. You do not find guilt, and you do not mete out punishment.

Conclusion

As a correctional officer, you must keep a proper perspective. You should develop a feel for the distinction between the sometimes confusing and occasionally tedious activities of a correctional officer and the always challenging and often rewarding role of the correctional officer. Keep your priorities in focus and do not be uncomfortable or dissatisfied with the limits of your authority. When the pressure is on and you have to make decisions and take actions in a split second that others will have the luxury of days and months to critique, remember the core of your duties:

1. Keep the public safe.

2. Keep the staff and inmates safe.

3. Meet basic needs and help enable change in inmates who are willing.

Styles of Control and Supervision

By Jess Maghan, Ph.D.

The style of supervision and control used by correctional officers is governed by agency policy and procedures and inmates' civil rights.

Today's correctional officers must be flexible and have the ability to communicate effectively. In the correctional system, new line staff are expected to assume immediate and full responsibility for the supervision and control of other people. The inherent discretionary power of correctional officers is apparent in their custodial duties. This power must be used to ensure a safe and secure environment.

Experienced correctional officers know how the environment of correctional facilities affects care, custody, and control. They are able to read the jail or prison climate for signs of unrest, fear, and danger. Officers and inmates have a mutual interest in maintaining a safe and secure correctional environment.

Training programs for correctional officers should be designed to strengthen interpersonal communication skills. Officers should be trained in cultural awareness and race relations, effective communication and listening skills, crisis intervention, methods to reduce violence and promote safety, and stress and anger management.

Jess Maghan, Ph.D., is associate commissioner of Training and Resource Development for the New York City Department of Correction.

The author acknowledges Captain Daphony P. Lyons and Correctional Officer Larry Patterson of the New York City Department of Correction for sharing their extensive experience in the custody and control of inmates.

Officers who use appropriate interpersonal communication techniques can effectively control and supervise today's growing and complex inmate population. There are more than 1.1 million inmates in U.S. jails and prisons (ACA 1990; ACA 1992). This growing population is the result of an increase in drug-related crime and is compounded by other social and economic problems. Today's inmates are likely to be young, racial minorities, uneducated, unafraid of punishment, and difficult to manage.

Fortunately, many correctional agencies are responding to the needs of correctional officers by providing them specialized training programs. Endeavors to lessen occupational stress are giving officers ownership in the institutional decision-making process. With this involvement, officers can heighten their role in having a positive affect on the conditions of confinement for inmates and on their own work environment. However, this also requires correctional officers to develop situational management skills.

Situational Management

Correctional officers will often need to motivate inmates to comply with orders. Motivating inmates requires a variety of skills. Successful correctional officers can control and predict inmate behavior. The style of supervision and control used by correctional officers is governed by agency policy and procedures and inmates' civil rights.

These variables constantly interact with variables of the physical environment of the correctional facility itself (e.g., facilities constructed specifically for, or renovated to accommodate, direct supervision, unit management, or punitive segregation, as well as facilities supporting open-dormitory or single-cell environments). In other words, people, physical plant, and program are the organizational dynamics that define supervision and control.

"Supervision is telling people, in face-to-face discussion, what to do and how to do it. Supervision, then, is the direct control over the performance of certain stated tasks. It is a means of issuing orders to individuals and ensuring that those orders are carried out. It is control by persuasion, suggestion and command" (Megginson 1967). In corrections, it is working with inmates to gain their cooperation in meeting the mission, goals, and objectives of a correctional agency.

As supervisors, correctional officers exhibit leadership by influencing inmates to strive willingly for the objectives of the agency. Leadership involves accomplishing correctional goals with the cooperation of inmates.

Correctional officers may influence inmates by either of two ways: (1) they tell inmates what to do and how to do it, or (2) they share their leadership responsibilities with inmates by involving them in the planning and execution of tasks. The former is known as authoritarian style of supervision, which emphasizes the completion of tasks; the latter is referred to as nondirective or democratic style of supervision, which stresses a cognizance for human differences and relationships (Megginson 1967).

In authoritarian supervision, an officer's power is derived from the officer's position of control and authority. The officer constitutes the center of authority and makes decisions without consulting inmates. Generally, correctional officers feel free to modify, evaluate, and interpret policies if such action can be justified through a written report. On the other hand, authoritarian correctional officers will insist inmates obey their orders without question. Officers will often use coercive power to get subordinates to complete tasks. Inmates must follow orders or face some type of negative reinforcement, such as a ticket for a rule infraction, loss of good time, or loss of some other privilege.

In democratic supervision, the correctional officer's power is acknowledged by inmates, and inmates, if properly motivated, can be self-directed and creative when given a task to complete. Correctional officers using the democratic supervision approach will consult with inmates to help them organize themselves into a productive scheme. Correctional officers in this case view themselves as team leaders.

Two types of team leadership styles to consider are bureaucratic and free-rein (Megginson 1967).

As a bureaucratic team leader, the correctional officer's source of power resides in correctional law, the power of the peace officers' state penal code, and agency rules and regulations. The officers' role is to carry out rules and regulations, court orders, consent decrees, and so on, with supervisors and command staff providing support and guidance.

On the other hand, the officer may opt for a free-rein style of leadership, which is based on individual inmates, their work knowledge, and dignity. Officers in this case do not make decisions for inmates; instead, they permit each member of the group to make his or her own decisions and permit the group to carry out decisions.

If officers were to rate their subordinates' performance of tasks (work details, job training, cooperation, etc.) on only two criteria, the criteria would most likely be (1) the ability to do the job and (2) the willingness to do the job. Officers' leadership style depends on the ability and willingness of inmates to complete assigned tasks and to take responsibility for directing their own behavior. From the situational leadership concept, four distinct categories of subordinates are derived (Hersey & Blanchard 1982):

- unable and unwilling inmate (e.g., an inmate who has just completed a detoxification program is given a work detail involving heavy lifting and straining, the inmate claims to be physically too weak and refuses to do the job)

- able and unwilling inmate (e.g., a detainee given a work assignment for which he is physically and mentally able to perform states that "as a detainee" he has the legal right to refuse to work)

- able and willing inmate (e.g., an inmate with average abilities and comprehension volunteers for an institutional program, such as shock incarceration or vocational training)

- unable and willing inmate (e.g., an inmate lacks the education, comprehension, and skill to complete given tasks, but is willing to learn and cooperate)

A different leadership style is needed for each category of subordinate, if not each individual inmate.

Supervising Unable and Unwilling Inmates

The authoritarian style of supervision works well with inmates who are unable and unwilling to obey orders. Officers must insist that their orders be obeyed while still being sensitive and understanding of inmates' pertinent problems and treating inmates respectfully. Officers should use their power (influence potential) to induce compliance. According to Hersey and Blanchard (1982), inmates in the unable and unwilling category are usually incompetent or lack confidence. Their unwillingness is usually the result of insecurity and uncertainty regarding the necessary tasks. Thus, a direct order or command that provides clear, specific directions and supervision is likely to be effective. The officer should tell the inmate what, when, how and where to do various tasks (Hersey & Blanchard 1982).

Supervising Able and Unwilling Inmates

Motivation and persuasion work when supervising able and unwilling inmates. In some cases, the inmates' unwillingness is the result of their lack of confidence or their insecurity; in other instances their unwillingness is a motivational problem. A supportive, but nondirective, participative style of supervision is effective in overcoming the inmate's unwillingness and gaining compliance.

The officer's personal power, which is acquired from inmates, other officers, and supervisors, also plays an important role. Personal power is shown in the extent to which followers are committed and loyal to their leader and the extent to which peers, supervisors, and subordinates allow themselves to be influenced by that individual (Etzioni 1961; Hersey & Blanchard 1982). The degree of personal power an individual has directly relates to the degree of influence others, by their own free choice, allow the individual to have on them. Personal power is acquired by virtue of the officer's personality, competence, and integrity. According to Hersey and Blanchard (1982), if an individual wants to influence another person's behavior, the individual must first understand what motivates that person.

Supervising Able and Willing Inmates

The free-rein style of leadership can be used effectively with inmates who are able and willing. According to Megginson (1967), the free-rein style is based on the individual's self-worth, knowledge, and dignity. The officer should provide little direction or support. The subordinate is free to run the show and decide how, when, and where the tasks should be completed.

Supervising Unable and Willing Inmates

A "selling approach" based on the bureaucratic leadership style should be used to supervise unable and willing inmates. Usually this type of inmate is confident, but lacks the skills to complete tasks. Officers should explain to the inmate that his or her willingness is appreciated, but that he or she lacks the skills necessary to do the task. Inmates will usually go along with officers' decisions if they understand the reasons for the decisions. Inmates view officers as carrying out policy, rules, and regulations of the agency. Inmates must know that officers have the support of facility supervisors and managers.

Building a Foundation for Effective Control and Supervision

The routine and regimentation inherent in correctional environments can wear down correctional officers. They become less vigilant and more susceptible to negative influences. Officers can prevent this "burnout" by learning from their environment and adhering to basic tenets of custody and supervision.

Tenets of Control and Supervision

When contemplating the tenets of control and supervision that follow, officers must keep in mind that they are constantly being observed by inmates. In this context, correctional officers present a role model to emulate or avoid.

1. Be neat and in proper uniform at all times.

2. Refrain from vulgarity and other inmate argot terms.

3. Know and obey the rules and regulations of the prison.

4. Apply the rules and regulations of the prison equally and fairly.

5. Refrain from discussing personal lives with inmates.

6. Be careful not to let inmates overhear conversations with other officers and staff.

7. Never make a promise to an inmate that cannot be delivered.

8. Be expert listeners.

9. Always listen beyond what is being verbally communicated by inmates.

10. Be credible and follow up on requests made by inmates.

These time-proven rules of conduct serve as a foundation for effective control and supervision of inmates. They suggest a way-of-being on the job that carries the opportunity for personal and professional empowerment.

Supervising Inmates

To use situational leadership effectively, officers should strive for respect (personal power), not popularity, among inmates. To achieve personal power, officers must have knowledge, skill, and expertise.

Correctional officers who supervise inmates effectively do the following:

1. Act like leaders by setting examples.

2. Treat inmates like human beings by being involved and concerned and showing respect.

3. Train and instruct, answer questions.

4. Know how to listen.

5. Give clear and realistic orders.

6. Keep abreast of what is going on in the housing areas.

7. Do not criticize inmates in front of other inmates.

8. Attempt to understand problems of the inmates.

Carnegie (1978) suggests that to effectively supervise individuals, supervisors should (1) guide individuals—ineffective supervisors drive individuals, (2) inspire enthusiasm rather than instill fear, and (3) rely on cooperation rather than on authority (depending on the situation).

Two major problems of leadership are illustrated by supervisors who are too lenient and those who are hard-boiled (Carnegie 1978). Easygoing officers try to please inmates and trust that their subordinates are doing the right thing. Minor rule infractions are often overlooked or ignored. These officers sometimes apologize for having to do their job. They use praise so frequently that it loses significance among inmates. As a result, little care is taken to provide services and security, and there is no discipline. Inmates may even arm themselves with homemade weapons because they feel that officers cannot protect them from other hostile and aggressive inmates.

On the other hand, hard-boiled supervisors may feel that they have to be tough and dogmatic to do their jobs and take the attitude that "I am the boss here." This approach may lead inmates to feel that they need to display their power to show that they deserve respect.

A balance between the two extremes must be found. The classical approach to inmate supervision is to be fair but firm. Officers should be assertive, but always consistent and fair, in their dealing with inmates (Lyons 1992).

Empowerment

Empowerment represents shaping an individual's natural leadership capacities to enhance his or her performance as a correctional officer. It is the ability to take full responsibility for hearing the problems of others without getting caught up emotionally in their predicaments. Personal empowerment is strengthened by working constantly to improve communication and listening skills, self-confidence, assertiveness, and physical and psychological presence on and off the job. This sense of empowerment guides officers to successful and rewarding careers.

The following ten points from the work philosophy statement of the 1991 Corrections Officer of the Year from the State of Illinois (Vaughn 1992) illustrate how a sense of personal and professional empowerment can lead to career fulfillment. Correctional officers should do the following:

1. Treat co-workers as equals.

2. Always try to do their job to the best of their ability and enjoy their work.

3. Keep it simple—do their job on the job and leave their job on the job.

4. Refrain from bringing personal problems to work.

5. Try to help co-workers—they should work with each other, not against each other.

6. Be proud of their uniform and their peace officer status—be conscious of their appearance, presence, and demeanor.

7. Participate in training and volunteer for special assignments.

8. Show respect to inmates, thereby earning the inmates' respect.

9. Be on time—attitude and attendance are directly related.

10. Develop friendships with those in the field or find a mentor so that they have someone to turn to when they feel alone and stressed-out on the job.

Correctional officers must learn to be self-determining through personal and professional empowerment and a sense of dignity. They must realize that inmate rights improve the rights of officers and that everyone can benefit from change. Correctional officers can take pride in their flexibility because it leads to the capacity to manage, control, and supervise the diverse group of inmates for whom they are responsible.

Officers in charge of the control and supervision of their personal lives will be able to control and supervise inmates under their remand. With this sense of empowerment, correctional officers truly appreciate the time-proven adage of "accepting the things they cannot change, courage to change the things they can . . . and the wisdom to know the difference."

References

American Correctional Association. 1992. *Juvenile and Adult Correctional Departments, Institutions, Agencies & Paroling Authorities Directory*. Laurel, Md.: ACA.

American Correctional Association. 1990. *National Jail & Adult Detention Directory*. Laurel, Md.: ACA.

Carnegie, D. 1978. *Managing through people*. New York: Simon and Schuster.

Etzioni, A. 1961. *A comprehensive analysis of complex organizations*. New York: The Free Press.

Hersey, P., and K. Blanchard. 1982. *Management of organizational behavior*. Englewood Cliffs, N.J.: Prentice Hall.

Lyons, D. P. 1992. Management by walking around (M.B.W.A.). *Keeper's Voice* 13 (April): 14–16.

Maghan, J. 1981. Guarding in prison. In *Justice as fairness—perspectives on the justice model*, D. Fogel and J. Hudson, eds. Cincinnati, Ohio: Anderson Publishing Company.

Megginson, L. C. 1967. *Personnel administration*. Chicago: Richard D. Irwin, Inc.

Vaughn, J. 1992. The Illinois 1991 correctional officer of the year. *Keeper's Voice* 13 (April): 17.

Racial Differences and the Supervision of Inmates

By Portia Hunt, Ph.D., and Liz Golden

Transcultural correctional officers have a basic under-standing of their own development as racial beings, and they can understand racial attitudes of other groups.

When communicating in a cross-cultural context, people tend to be spontaneous and assume that their style of interacting is universal. They believe that everyone applies the same meaning to an encounter. At the same time, most of us recognize that cultural differences exist.

Changing demographics and shifts in the political and social climate have inspired professionals in many fields to look at how and when assumptions about race and culture affect their perceptions and behavior on the job. Those who work in the justice system have begun to take on this challenge. In this chapter, we will look at the ways racial identity issues and racial differences—particularly between blacks and whites—might affect the work of correctional officers, why these issues may be difficult to sort out, and some theoretical models that can be useful in developing greater cultural competency in the supervision of inmates.

A Balanced Perspective

In the past four decades, the justice system has responded to social and political pressure to humanize correctional institutions by

Portia Hunt, Ph.D., is a professor at Temple University and the president of Eclipse Management Consultant Group, which is based in Philadelphia, Pennsylvania .

Liz Golden is the associate director of marketing and development for Eclipse Management Consultant Group.

focusing on rehabilitation rather than punishment. This shift has recast the job of "guard" to that of correctional officer, thus professionalizing the role and expanding its functions to include supervision, counseling, and performance evaluation. Increased awareness of systemic inequities based on race, ethnicity, and class has led professionals at all levels of the justice system to study the incidence of minority over-representation in corrections and its implications for specific job functions.

These structural changes and social trends have led to confusion over the appropriate approach toward the supervision of inmates. On one hand are "old guard" personnel who view their role as that of an "enforcer" who ensures prison rules are enforced and inmates are securely confined. This punitive approach to supervision is based on the belief that inmates have committed crimes and should be appropriately disciplined, regardless of their emotional or personal needs.

On the other hand are "social work" personnel who view their role very differently, seeing themselves as advocates who can help inmates learn to be productive members of society once they've served their time. This rehabilitative approach is based on the belief that inmates are perpetrators of crimes, but they are also victims of poverty, abuse, racism, and poor education.

Old-timers often perceive rehabilitation negatively, viewing staff who take the social work approach as ineffective and too soft on inmates. The justice system has tried to achieve a balance between these two models by recognizing that both are necessary. Now, the professional correctional officer has the responsibility to both guard inmates and advocate on their behalf.

Correctional officers who come from a traditional law-and-order framework and who see themselves as guards might have difficulty understanding the need for training in human relations and cross-cultural communication, because from their perspective, handling problems and keeping order is a matter of quick action and maintaining control, rather than negotiation or conflict resolution. Crisis situations can develop quickly, and correctional officers often have little time to think about how to respond. Nevertheless, the ability to communicate and evaluate both verbal and nonverbal behavior in a cross-cultural or interracial context could make these quick judgments more accurate and effective.

Gaps in the training and reeducation process, which only recently has come to include training in human relations, cross-cultural communication, and mediation, add to conflicts in ideology and role function. Insufficient skills combined with personality conflicts could increase the likelihood of problems on the job. For example, correctional officers may unintentionally intensify conflicts by unnecessarily challenging inmates. This happens frequently with correctional officers who have a strong need to save face or who use their position to abuse power. Because they are unwilling to admit that they don't know how to handle a given situation, they may keep inmates in their place by flexing their muscles to show who's in charge.

On the other hand, there are those who are uncomfortable with conflict and the power dynamics of the prison setting. Viewing their role as supportive, they run the risk of allowing a volatile situation to explode.

While the traditional guard may not see the merit of developing communications skills and the newcomer may not appreciate the importance of enforcing rules, comprehensive training and a balanced perspective is critical to the work of correctional officers if they are to accurately and fairly assess inmates' performance and motivation. Adding an awareness of racial and cultural issues to already stressful and highly demanding work will, in many ways, increase the complexities of the correctional officer's work. However, failure to take these factors into account may result in conflicts among inmates and among correctional officers, worse, inmates may become polarized around race.

Who Are the Inmates?

A high proportion of inmates in correctional institutions are likely to be male, African American, young adults, poorly educated, and from inner city communities. The number of Hispanic males entering the system is smaller but increasing. Women represent only a small proportion of the inmate population.

Because many inmates bring with them social problems and poor coping skills that are endemic to growing up in poverty, they are predisposed to misinterpreting and misunderstanding interpersonal dynamics and may exhibit short tempers, impulsivity, distorted thinking, paranoia, and violence.

Understanding the history of racial oppression and violence against people of color by whites—as well as the complexities of the development of racial identity, interracial dynamics, and conflict—can help separate inappropriate inmate behavior from behavior based on legitimate concerns about racism and conflict.

The Importance of Racial Identity

Personality development is multifaceted and proceeds over time with varying periods of intensity, depending on the circumstances of our lives. Racial identity develops much like other aspects of identity. Our perceptions of ourselves and others are shaped, to some extent, by how we perceive ourselves racially.

According to racial identity development theorists, people have a wide range of attitudes about belonging to their racial group (Cross 1971; Helms 1990). These attitudes depend on the individual's relationships, personal experiences, and world view and whether his or her views confer with, move against, or are different from the views held by the sociopolitical majority. Identity is unique, fluid, and variable. Indeed, there are more differences among members of a racial group than between members of different racial groups. However, organizing identity development into discrete stages is useful in understanding patterns of behavior. The following are two models of racial identity development and how they affect interactions between correctional officers and inmates.

Minority Identity Development Model

The minority identity development model developed by Atkinson, Morten, and Sue (1979) is an outgrowth of the earlier Theory of Nigrescence model developed by Cross (1971). Although the model as discussed here focuses on identity development of African Americans, it can be generalized to other cultural/social/political minorities (Asian Americans, Latinos, gays, women, etc.).

If a dominant racial group has strong negative views about a minority group and has reinforced these negative views through years of socialization, then a segment of that minority group will internalize those negative stereotypes and view the dominant group in appreciative, positive ways. This rejection of one's racial group is called *conformity*, indicating conformity with the dominant group's evaluation of them. Whites, the dominant group in the United States, may prefer blacks who conform because they don't make waves.

All ethnic minority groups have derogatory names for members they feel have bought into the negative stereotypes about their group. Other blacks will think of the conformist as an "Uncle Tom" or an "oreo" (black on the outside, white on the inside) because they see the display of internalized racist, white norms and attitudes as a betrayal of black identity.

If a significant incident or group of incidents force black individuals in conformity to challenge their internalized negative stereotypes, they may find themselves angry, confused, and conflicted about the way their group is regarded by whites. This conflict signals *dissonance*, a phase of active questioning where the once-accepted negative attitudes toward blacks are tentatively challenged and the previously unquestioned positive attitudes toward whites are confronted.

As new experiences evoke increasing concern and anger at racist norms and a deeper appreciation for a positive racial identity, black individuals are likely to move into an active rejection of dominant cultural norms and of whites. The Civil Rights movement acted as a catalyst to push many blacks out of confusion and into rejection of whites as racial oppressors and the unilateral acceptance of themselves as racial beings.

This is characterized by immersion into the study of their racial/cultural group's heritage, contributions, oppression, etc., and the rejection of and emergence from depreciation by the dominant culture. In this *resistance and immersion* phase, distrust and rage toward whites are the primary emotions. Typically, whites respond to this phase with fear, anger, and denial and often label blacks and other minority group members in resistance and immersion as militant.

If black individuals establish contact with some whites whom they have learned to trust, or if they maintain close relationships with other blacks who have white friends, they start what can be a painful questioning of the unilateral acceptance/rejection paradigm. Discomforted by the rigid views held in the resistance and immersion phase, they begin to explore the basis for rejecting all white people and accepting all black people. Once the questioning has commenced, identity development shifts into a phase of *introspection.* In this phase the black person realizes that some individual whites can be trusted and that it is necessary to discriminate between the individual and the group. At the same time, there is still recognition of systemic racism and the effect it can have on the behavior and attitude of whites.

Synergy, the fifth phase, is characterized by resolution of the discomfort experienced in the previous phase; there is a greater sense of individual choice and flexibility. The person values his or her own racial/ethnic group and can communicate with whites and other ethnic minorities, making an objective evaluation of the existence and value of their cultural differences.

Minority Identity Development and Correctional Officer/Inmate Supervision

There are many instances where a correctional officer's self-evaluation and informal assessment of an inmate's stage of racial identity could be useful in understanding dynamics between that inmate and the correctional officer or between that inmate and other inmates. For example, if a black inmate is particularly compliant with a white correctional officer, it may be that the inmate is at the conformity stage of racial identity development. Depending on the correctional officer's own identity development, the inmate's behavior could be interpreted in dramatically different ways. A white correctional officer might view the black inmate as cooperative, appropriately subservient, and ideally behaved. A black correctional officer who is in the resistance and immersion phase, however, may view that inmate as untrustworthy and an Uncle Tom. Thus, the inmate would be evaluated and treated differently by the two correctional officers even though the inmate's behavior is consistent.

In another example, if a black inmate is in the resistance and immersion phase, he or she will most likely reject all whites and will unconditionally value blacks, especially those who are Afrocentric. To demonstrate racial loyalty and the concomitant rejection of whites and white culture, the inmate may become a Black Muslim. If the correctional officer is black and also in resistance and immersion, the inmate may feel a sense of solidarity with the correctional officer and may go along with his or her directives. If the black correctional officer is in the conformity phase, the inmate may feel resentful and may be uncooperative. This inmate would probably be resistant to any white correctional officer.

These examples of how minority identity development can affect behavior and perspective have been simplified for the purpose of illustration; it is important to remember that every situation is complex, and there are many factors impinging on the evolution of the actions and attitudes of both inmates and correctional officers. Nevertheless, examining these dynamics can help explain why a particular inmate will be treated in dramatically different ways by inmates and correctional officers and why that inmate may be evaluated in opposing ways.

Racial Identity of Whites and Majority Groups

"... It is still possible [for whites] to exist without ever having to acknowledge [their] racial identity" (Helms 1990: 54). In fact, whites frequently see minority groups as the only ones with racial identities. White people's unawareness of their racial identity and its accompanying set of cultural norms can create the myopia of monoculturalism that makes them think that their way of perceiving or interpreting interpersonal communication is the right way or the normal way.

Most white correctional officers are unaware that the institutional norms that govern their functioning are developed, for the most part, around white, Anglo-Saxon, Protestant values. They assume that their systems and decisions are racially neutral, objective, and without a cultural perspective.

"The development of white identity in the United States is closely intertwined with the development and progress of racism in this country" (Helms 1990: 49). Whites, as well as minorities, are socialized into racism and their racial identity. The dramatic difference is that whites receive power and privilege as part and parcel of the process, whereas minorities obviously do not. At first questioning most whites do not endorse racist behavior and ideology. However, the process of developing a deeply rooted positive racial identity that includes eliminating internalized racism is a complex process that involves more than claiming, "I am not a racist."

The various transitions whites experience as they learn to recognize and abandon overt and covert racism and as they explore what it means to be white and nonracist in our culture involves two broad phases: the abandonment of racism and the establishment of a positive white identity (Carter & Helms 1987; Helms 1984). Each phase has three interrelated stages.

Abandoning Racism

The first stage, *contact*, is characterized by denial, naivete, and ignorance about the effect of race on social/political power and interpersonal dynamics. The typical comments made by whites in the contact stage are "People are people," "I don't see color," and "I treat everybody the same." Beneath the naive, "colorblind" stance, however, is a tacit acceptance of racial inequality.

If white individuals make and sustain contact with African Americans, they will soon become aware that race relations are in fact a problem and that black people have a different view of the topic. They may also acknowledge for the first time that their naive comments are offensive to black people. As contact continues, the developing relationship begins to shake up the white person's belief system. Feelings of anxiety about present entitlement and racial injustices, guilt about past race relations, and resentment about being made aware of racial tensions may surface. The white individual will become uncomfortable when discussing racial issues around blacks, and likewise, will feel uncomfortable if he or she is in social situations with only a few blacks and many whites. This dissembling of innocence about racism is called the *disintegration* stage. To repress the accompanying strong emotions, the white individual may show solidarity with blacks by trying to imitate them or by developing a paternalistic attitude toward the group. Both strategies are designed to reduce guilt and anxiety and to gain acceptance by blacks. Unfortunately, the combination of paternalism and a questioning of the status quo is likely to result in rejection by both blacks and whites.

If the cross-racial relationship is maintained or if the white person works in an integrated setting, the anxiety of disintegration will likely be heightened, and the emotional discomfort will push the white person to internally manipulate his or her new awareness of race to fit back into the terms of racism. Although it may not be clearly conscious, the central concern during this stage is loss of entitlements. This stage, called *reintegration*, is a reactionary one, and is a form of intellectually formulated racism that will be expressed in what on the surface may look like objective terms. An overt and dramatic expression of reintegration is the forming of white supremist groups.

If the white person maintains contact with a black person or if he or she has white friends who are at a higher stage of racial consciousness, then the person's racist attitudes can be challenged. When the challenge is successful, the person is ready to move into phase two: the establishment of a positive white identity.

Establishing a Positive White Identity

The first stage of this phase is *pseudo-independence*, indicating the introduction of a white identity that is developing outside of racist social norms. The person at this stage understands racism intellectually, recognizes institutionalized racism, and is able to acknowledge his or her own racism and white privilege; there is a willingness to challenge racism and a strong desire to eradicate the effects of racial oppression by idealizing blacks, learning about black culture and the effects of racism, and helping blacks get through the system by showing them how to act white. Whites at this stage will still experience the guilt associated with the awareness of entitlement, but in the context of acknowledging the larger, systemic problem, the guilt is tolerable.

If the white person has continued to develop cross-racial relationships or is connected to whites who are also struggling with racism, then the person may enter the *immersion/emersion* stage, which is characterized by a less guilty acceptance of white identity and a deeper understanding of the dynamics of personal and institutional racism. Here, there is a deep recognition that whites need to take responsibility for creating and maintaining racism. What ensues is movement away from studying the experience of minorities and an immersion into the cultural experiences of whites who have explored the insidious effects of racism on their lives and who have worked to overcome it in a meaningful way. The white person at this stage is comfortable enough with his or her identity to begin discussing racism with black friends and can tolerate hearing negative things about whites from blacks.

The final stage, *autonomy* (or transculturalism), is distinguished by the recognition that other racial/ethnic groups are different, but not inferior or deficient. Intimacy is possible across groups. Openness to accept and develop intimate friendships with people from different racial groups is supported by a broader consciousness of power dynamics and cultural values. Transcultural whites display an understanding of racism in institutions and in their personal lives and feel self-acceptance as white people.

White Racial Identity and Correctional Officer/Inmate Supervision

There are many circumstances where looking at white racial identity can provide the missing link that explains behavior or will deescalate a brewing conflict.

White inmates in the contact stage will experience a high degree of anxiety and stress (as will white correctional officers) if they are in an institution that is predominantly black. If they express their naivete openly, they may find themselves in conflict with black inmates by virtue of making seemingly innocent comments that are interpreted by blacks as racist. The white correctional officer who is in pseudo-independence or autonomy can help the contact stage inmate (or correctional officer) understand the racial context in cross-racial settings. A black correctional officer in introspection or synergy can also assist the white inmate. On the other hand, a black correctional officer who is in the stage of resistance and immersion may experience some irritation toward this inmate, regardless of the inmate's behavior.

If the white inmate is in reintegration, overt or covert racist attitudes will prevail. He or she will probably have antagonistic or hostile relations with black inmates and will likely stay racially isolated. At the extreme, he or she may join white supremist groups to express rejection of blacks and to claim white identity. Any black correctional officer will be at a disadvantage when trying to communicate with this inmate. A white correctional officer may be more able to elicit cooperation.

If the white correctional officer is in reintegration, he or she may be covert in expressing racist views to other correctional officers, but inmates are likely to pick up on the correctional officer's racism. Correctional officers at this stage could probably find many ways to justify poor evaluation of black inmates or of white inmates who show alliance with blacks.

Importance of Racial Identity for Correctional Officers

Awareness of racial identity development can help correctional officers make accurate evaluations of many situations that might arise on the job. For example, where they may once have automatically dismissed an inmate's claim of systemic racism as an effort to excuse failure or as a way to avoid taking responsibility for an action, correctional officers who are astute about racial issues are better equipped to discriminate between inmates who have legitimate concerns and those who may be manipulating the correctional officer for other reasons. Further, they are in a better position to communicate with the inmate about what may be going on.

Understanding interracial relationships in terms of racial identity development also gives correctional officers a common language with which to communicate and to evaluate their actions and judgments. Because correctional officers undergo the same conflict around belonging to their racial group as the inmates they supervise, they will need to struggle with and clarify their own racial identity issues. Otherwise, they may feel pulled apart and make dramatic errors in judgment; their professional responsibilities will collide with their racial self-concept.

Handling Conflict

An inmate's interpretation of a correctional officer's decisions in resolving conflicts, making evaluations, or interacting in general can either restore peace or lead to further problems. Whether or not an inmate's assumptions about a correctional officer's intervention are accurate, the correctional officer's ignorance about cultural differences, power dynamics, and how racial group members are likely to interpret his or her behavior may leave the officer open for unwanted pressure to demonstrate fairness along racial lines or may unconsciously escalate racial tensions.

White Correctional Officer and Black and White Inmate Conflict

In a situation where a white correctional officer is called on to resolve a conflict between a black inmate and a white inmate, if the correctional officer sides with the white inmate, black inmates will probably think the white correctional officer is racist and showing preferential treatment for his or her own race. White inmates will probably think the correctional officer was being fair and not taking sides.

Should the correctional officer side with the black inmate, he or she may be viewed by blacks as an ally who rose above racism, while white inmates will probably think the officer is a sell out.

Black Correctional Officer and Black and White Inmate Conflict

In the situation where the correctional officer is black and the combating inmates are white and black, if the correctional officer sides with the white inmate, the black inmate is likely to feel that the correctional officer is a traitor to his or her own race. White inmates will think the correctional officer is being fair and nonbiased.

If the correctional officer sides with the black inmate, whites will feel that the officer is showing favoritism to his or her own racial group. Black inmates will praise the correctional officer for having courage to "buck the system."

Black Correctional Officer and Black Inmate Conflict

If a black correctional officer has to intervene when two black inmates are in conflict, the inmates may or may not interpret the correctional officer's behavior within a racial context. Instead, the correctional officer's personality and style of handling conflict will emerge as a key factor in how the intervention will be perceived. If the correctional officer has a "macho" personality and uses excessive force to intervene, he may be viewed as the "white man's token," or as a "white man in black skin." The correctional officer is seen as having to "outwhite whitey" on the job.

If the correctional officer is even-handed and conveys a desire to be fair as well as acknowledging an awareness of himself or herself as a racial being, black inmates will view the officer as belonging to the race and as being compassionate but fair.

White Correctional Officer and White Inmate Conflict

In striking contrast, when a conflict between two white inmates is settled by a white correctional officer, the officer's action is rarely interpreted in a racial context. This is primarily because whites do not think of themselves as racial beings because as the social/political majority, there appears to be no need.

A No-win Situation

In many instances correctional officers are caught between a rock and a hard place when mediating or handling conflicts. If they side with inmates of their race they are heros to their racial group and automatically biased against the other race. If they side with inmates from the other racial groups, they are traitors within their own group and champions of race relations with other racial groups.

Conclusion

Understanding the evolution of racial identity for minorities and for the sociopolitical majority (whites) will shed some light on the complex dynamics of race that may be shaping perception and behavior in the prison setting.

Transcultural correctional officers have a basic understanding of their own development as racial beings, and they can understand racial attitudes of other groups. This prepares correctional officers to discuss racial issues as they affect inmates, the institution, and the justice system without being defensive or protective.

Transcultural correctional officers are powerfully equipped to develop skills in managing diversity, deescalating racial conflicts, and predicting when inmates are likely to reject their assistance. They can evaluate the importance of race for any given action or interaction and discern when inmates are being misinterpreted or mistreated by those in power. Mutual awareness of racial dynamics gives correctional officers the opportunity to rely on each other to intervene when racial differences may be preventing inmates or correctional officers from effectively communicating.

References

Atkinson, D., G. Morten, and C. Sue. 1979. *Counseling American minorities: A cross-cultural perspective*. Dubuque, Iowa: W.C. Brown Co.

Carter, R. T., and J. E. Helms. 1987. The relationship between black value orientations and racial identity attitudes: Measurements and evaluations. *Counseling & Development* 19 (4): 185–95.

Cross, W. E., Jr. 1971. The Negro-to-Black conversion experience: Toward a psychology of Black liberation. *Black World* 29 (9): 13–27.

Helms, J. E. 1984. Toward a theoretical explanation of the effects of race on counseling: A black and white model. *The Counseling Psychologist* 12 (4): 153–165.

Helms, J. E. 1990. *Black and white racial identity*. New York: Greenwood Press.

Kochman, T. 1984. *Black & white styles in conflict*. Chicago, Ill.: University of Chicago Press.

Keys to Effective Inmate Management: Avoiding Manipulation

By Lt. Gary F. Cornelius

> *When an officer falls victim to manipulation, a small, but significant, crack appears in the security system of the institution.*

"I should have known better!"

"I've been suckered again!"

"They got over on me again!"

Just about all correctional officers have expressed similar feelings of frustration after being manipulated, or conned, by inmates. When officers are manipulated by inmates, they feel cheated and used. Their morale may suffer, and they may experience extreme stress. They may feel disillusioned because, as professionals, they want to help inmates help themselves, but being conned makes them wonder whether their efforts are wasted.

When an officer falls victim to manipulation, a small, but significant, crack appears in the security system of the institution. When inmates manipulate officers to bring in drugs, weapons, or unauthorized messages, the results can be serious. Escapes may occur; officers or inmates may be hurt or killed. By having contraband, inmates can control cellblocks with power they should not have.

Lt. Gary F. Cornelius is with the Fairfax County Sheriff's Office Community Corrections Division in Fairfax, Virginia, and is a consultant on issues in corrections.

Correctional officers will always be the targets of inmate con games. Whether you work in a prison, jail, halfway house, prerelease center, or juvenile detention center, as a correctional officer, your job is to control what inmates do, what they have, and where they go inside the institution. No one likes to live in this kind of environment. Consequently, inmates will always try to "get over" on you and make you do their bidding. Inmates try to trick correctional officers who, in turn, try to resist such manipulation. This presents a never-ending battle.

I have worked in corrections for almost fifteen years—in confinement, classification, and community corrections. My years of experience have taught me that inmates will always try to fool correctional officers. This chapter shares what I have learned about manipulation through my years in the field. It discusses inmate culture, techniques inmates use to manipulate officers, and ways officers can prevent manipulation from happening.

The Inmates' Culture

Inmates have a different moral code than the code followed by law-abiding citizens; they live by a different set of values. Many inmates have done time before and are experienced at surviving while incarcerated. In turn, they undergo "prisonization" (Allen 1991). Prisonization is the process whereby inmates adapt to and learn the customs, rules, and culture of other inmates in the institution, as well as the institution's regulations.

While adapting, inmates learn that deception, or manipulation, is important for survival (Johnson 1987). Similar to survival on the street—where they learned to use people—survival on the inside is crucial. Inmates want to do their time without any trouble.

If this manipulative behavior is combined with typical inmate behavior, such as impatience, irresponsibility, and a lack of values, the result is an immature person who survives by using others (Perdue 1983).

In the world of the inmate, there are a few basic rules.

1. Inmates want to do their time as easily and comfortably as possible (Irwin 1970). In the book, *In the Belly of the*

Beast: Letters from Prison, inmate Jack Abbot says, "the working code of a convict is at bottom to best the man, the pig [officer]. To do what he can to get his time done and get out of prison."

2. Inmates do not inform on each other. Generally they are close-mouthed, especially when an officer is investigating a rule violation.

3. Inmates avoid developing a cooperative relationship with officers. Inmates who show loyalty to fellow inmates are respected in jails or prisons. Staff, especially correctional officers, are to be resisted and opposed (Irwin 1980).

4. Inmates believe in their version of the Golden Rule, which is "Do Unto Others, But Do It First" (Johnson 1987). Inmates may go after an enemy first.

5. Inmates believe in being "solid," (Sands 1964) or resisting pressure from staff, and being loyal to other inmates.

Inmates' culture implies that only the strongest survive (Wojda et al. 1991). An image of strength is to be displayed. Emotions and feelings are not to be shown. Weak inmates and staff are to be preyed on, exploited, and used.

Manipulation Defined

The dictionary defines manipulation as "control or change especially by artful or unfair means so as to achieve a desired end."

Inmates want to control their world. When they see something they want—a cell change, trustee job, or a special visit—they attempt to control the situation. They want changes on their terms. For example, an inmate might see a chance to transfer to a cellblock as an opportunity to exploit weak inmates. Or an inmate might con a counselor into giving him a library trustee job so he can run drugs throughout the prison.

Inmates can be great actors and actresses when they want something. For example, an inmate might arrange for his girlfriend to bring in drugs. To do this, he has to get approval for a special "contact" visit. He concocts a story about having suicidal thoughts or about his girlfriend being ill. He tells the fictitious tale to his classification counselor, who, moved by the inmate's "sincerity" supplemented by tears, approves the visit and unknowingly clears the way for drugs to be passed to the inmate during the visit.

An inmate's deception may also involve family members or friends of the inmate who agree to be part of a plan to manipulate an officer. For example, an inmate may tell his wife to call the counseling office with a fabricated story about their child being sick. Then, the counselor gets a request from the inmate for extra phone calls or for a transfer to administrative segregation, which is less stressful.

Correctional officers must ask themselves, "What does the inmate really want?" or "What is the intention of the inmate's request?" An inmate could want contraband, power over other inmates, or simply a break from the boring routine of prison life. Sometimes the desired end is to make you work for them without your knowing it.

Methods of Manipulation

Inmates use a variety of methods to manipulate officers. One is the "set-up" (Allen & Bosta 1981). "Setting up" an officer means that the inmate has purposely chosen the officer to be manipulated. This occurs for different reasons. Perhaps the officer has trouble saying no to inmates. Or the officer is sloppy in appearance and work habits, which tells the inmate that the officer does not pay a lot of attention to detail. Consequently, the officer may not check details of or verify an inmate's request. For example, an inmate's request to make several phone calls to his mother because she is ill and in the hospital should be followed up with questions such as, "What hospital?" and "What type of illness?" The officer should also personally check out the story's validity.

Set-ups can also be engineered by groups of inmates. Through the inmate "grapevine," knowledge gathered about the officer is analyzed by the inmate group before the officer is approached for the final manipulation.

The main thrust of the "con game" can take many forms— from "buttering you up," to sympathizing with you about a personal problem, to asking for help that supposedly only you can give. Another popular method is to "divide and conquer" the staff. Inmates may tell an officer that his or her supervisor was overheard saying that the officer in question runs a sloppy post. The hope here is that the officer will view the inmates as "friends" who watch out for him or her.

Regardless of how inmates choose to manipulate officers, the inmates' objective is to make the officer bend the rules, do something against procedure to help them, or look the other way. Such demands may include asking the officer to look the other way while an inmate passes a note to another inmate in a restricted area; to allow extra phone calls, visits, or recreation time; to allow people on the outside to bring in contraband; or to bring in drugs or weapons.

Why don't officers refuse or say no? Some find it difficult to say no because they fear they will offend inmates. Inmates see this as a weakness to be exploited. Correctional officers must learn to say no when appropriate.

By initially giving in to inmate manipulation, officers give inmates a handle, or lever, to use to control them (Allen & Bosta 1981). For example, a good-hearted, but misguided, correctional officer may give in and allow an inmate to pass messages to an inmate in another housing area, which is against the rules. After a few weeks of this, the inmate demands that the officer bring in a package from his wife without searching it. He tells the officer that he or she has been allowing rules to be broken all along; do it, or he will tell the officer's supervisor. The inmate now has a handle on the officer.

Some officers may feel that giving in to an inmate on a minor matter is just a one-time thing. Do not be fooled—it is not. Inmates will ask over and over again. They do not let go easily.

Avoiding Manipulation

To prevent manipulation, correctional officers must remember that they are always possible targets for set-ups, because inmate manipulation will always be part of the job. The following is a list of practical guidelines to help you guard against being conned. Although nothing you can do will ensure you will not be manipulated, by following some good advice, you can keep those instances to a minimum.

1. Educate yourself about inmates. To deal effectively with inmates, you must learn their culture. The references listed at the end of this chapter can help get you started.

2. Remember to be professional. Being a professional means that you perform a "valued and highly regarded function" (Stinchcombe 1986). As a correctional officer, there are things you can do to project a professional image to inmates. Keep a neat, sharp appearance. Know your department's code of ethics or code of conduct. Know your job; do not allow inmates to dictate your job to you. Keep confidential information about procedures, inmates, and staff to yourself. Do not gossip or spread rumors. Most important, keep a professional distance from inmates. They are incarcerated offenders in your care. They are not your "buddies" or your friends.

3. Be firm and in control. When working a post, you are the boss. You control your post—inmates do not. Learn how to say no. Set limits on your availability to inmates. See them on your terms, not theirs. Be firm, but be fair. Do not show favoritism; instead, strive to treat all inmates equally.

4. Communicate with other staff and your supervisor and document your actions. If you think you are being manipulated or are being looked on as a possible target, discuss this situation with your supervisor. Document incidents in logs, files, and memos. Let the inmate know that you are aware. Once the inmate realizes you are aware of the situation, the game is up (Allen & Bosta 1981).

5. Communicate clearly to the inmate. Inmates have a tendency to twist your words around. Make sure that when you talk to inmates, especially when you give them instructions, they understand you and your position.

6. If you are manipulated or victimized as a result of violated rules, admit your wrongdoing. If you tell your supervisor and "come clean," the disciplinary action taken might not be as severe as if you had denied your involvement or kept

quiet. Although you may be disciplined, a good supervisor will respect you for coming forward and admitting to your mistakes.

7. Get the details. If an inmate presents you with a problem or request, especially if it concerns the outside, such as death or illness in the family, get the details. Find out who, where, when, how, and where you can call for more information. If the problem is in the institution, such as a request for a transfer, investigate. Tell the inmate that you will check it out and will get back to him or her. An inmate may be taken off guard because you want to check things out. You may catch the inmate in a lie. Consult with your supervisor. Do not be too quick to make a decision.

In addition to these guidelines, "self-talks" will help you keep your guard up. Self-talks involve asking yourself questions such as, "If I grant this request, am I violating procedure?" and "What does this inmate really want?"

Although officers must be alert to possible manipulation by inmates, they must remember that not all inmates are out to manipulate officers when they want to speak to them or make a request. Some have a legitimate need for assistance. If all inmates are "brushed off" because officers mistakenly believe they are lying, inmates who really need help will not get it. One of the challenges of being a correctional officer is determining whether an inmate is being sincere or deceptive.

Conclusion

The culture of the inmate dictates survival. One way to survive is to manipulate the correctional officer, who controls the environment. The artistry of manipulation takes many forms and may involve other inmates and people on the outside. There are, however, some steps that correctional officers can take to protect themselves.

Working in corrections can be a rewarding and interesting career. If you remember that you are always a possible target for manipulation and you keep yourself informed and alert, you will be able to protect yourself from manipulation.

References

Abbot, J. 1981. *In the belly of the beast: Letters from prison.* New York: Vintage Books.

Allen, B., and D. Bosta. 1981. *Games criminals play and how you can profit by knowing them.* 2d Edition. Susanville, Calif.: Rae John.

Allen, H., and C. Simonsen. 1992. *Corrections in America: An introduction.* 6th Edition. New York: MacMillan.

Irwin, J. 1970. *The felon.* Englewood Cliffs, N.J.: Prentice Hall.

————. 1980. *Prisons in turmoil.* Boston: Little, Brown.

Johnson, R. 1987. *Hard time: Understanding and reforming the prison.* Monterey, Calif.: Brooks-Cole.

Sands, B. 1964. *My shadow ran fast.* 4th Edition. New York: Signet.

Stinchcombe, J. 1986. Correctional officer professionalism: Are the benefits worth the risk? *Journal of Correctional Training* 2 (3): 16-19.

Wojda, G., et al. 1991. *Behind bars.* Laurel, Md.: American Correctional Association.

Hostage Situations

By Dennis H. Sherman

It is important for correctional officers to know and understand strategies and techniques that affect captives so that they can play more effective roles in emergencies by understanding the recovery process.

One of the most serious and feared consequences of working in a prison is being involved in a hostage situation. This chapter examines how hostage negotiation can successfully end hostage situations.

When discussing hostage situations, the word "captive" is preferred over the word "hostage" because it is less provoking. Language training is an important technique used by negotiators in recovering captives safely in captive situations. Words, phrases, and strategies that bring minimal attention to captives are used to recover them safely.

Correctional officers may be taken captive any time, any place, any where by inmates for a variety of reasons. Emergencies, escapes, or disturbances can trigger such situations. Inmates may take staff in desperation or to gain concessions or status in the eyes of other inmates. A suicidal or emotionally disturbed inmate could take staff or other inmates captive. Whatever the situation, effective security procedures and close scrutiny of inmates can minimize the opportunities for captive takings to occur. In correctional facilities throughout the nation, good training, practiced captive negotiation response, and effective prison management have prevented significant injuries or death.

Dennis H. Sherman is a trainer and consultant in hostage negotiation and disturbance management for corrections and the law enforcement community.

Effective Prison Management

Effective prison management of crisis situations and emergencies makes it clear to inmates that captive takings and riots will result in criminal prosecution wherever possible and not in freedom, immunity, or amnesty. Such management implies that correctional employees who are taken captive do not have authority to negotiate. Correctional officers have accepted the risks that go along with working in a correctional institution, jail, or prison as part of their job. For these reasons, inmates think twice about taking captives.

The Objective of Negotiation

The objective of negotiation during captive takings is the safe recovery of captives. The goal is the same for both the tactical and the negotiation teams, which work together during the crisis. Good emergency response plans should clearly indicate that if captives are being harmed, assault may be ordered, provided that intelligence, information, and personnel are available. Continued monitoring of the well-being of the captives is of primary importance.

Captive Takings

Emergencies and captive takings can occur at any time. Front line correctional officers may be in the wrong place at the wrong time and may witness a captive taking, be held captive, or be close to the emergency. Moreover, they may be the first to respond to the incident and find an inmate who has taken a captive.

In this case, the captive taking should be reported immediately. It is important to be calm and observant. Officers should note the number of captors and their demands, as well as the number of captives, number and extent of injuries, number and type of weapons, keys, or radios taken, location, time, and other relevant items. The area of the emergency needs to be contained and isolated. The officers' safety and the safety of those around them is critical.

Time Is on the Captive's Side

Once negotiations begin, all available resources will be devoted to recovery of captives and making the institution safe and secure. Captive takings may not be resolved quickly. If force is not used immediately and if captives are unharmed, negotiation may continue for some time.

Usually, the most dangerous time for captives is when the riot or captive taking first takes place—generally during the first thirty minutes—and when a tactical assault occurs. However, as long as they are unharmed, time is on the side of the captives—not the captors. The uneventful passage of time allows negotiation to work and wear down the captors. A wait-and-negotiate approach in many captive takings improves the chances for safe recovery.

Captive Negotiation

Negotiation should not enhance the position of the captors. Accepting captor demands needs to be carefully thought out and part of a planned strategy. Weapons, drugs, or alcohol should not be given to captors. The negotiation process will attempt to get captives in return for concessions, such as food, drink, heat, or light.

Negotiation should be carried out by trained negotiators, who once on the scene will probably replace correctional officers or other staff initially involved in negotiation. Outsiders, such as the media, the public, or religious leaders, should only be used in negotiating at the discretion of trained negotiators. The only hard, fast rule in the negotiation process is "never say never." Every negotiation requires proper technique and flexibility to deal with the unexpected.

Because captive negotiation is complex, it requires a lot of training and practice. It is important for correctional officers to know and understand strategies and techniques that affect captives so that they can play more effective roles in emergencies by understanding the recovery process.

Bonding and the Stockholm Effect

In many captive situations, a bond, or closeness, develops between captors and captives. During life-threatening situations, captives begin to feel uncertain, guilty, helpless, humiliated, and depressed. They feel powerless and completely dependent on the captor for all needs. Even bodily needs, food, and water are all dependent on the benevolence of the captor. This life-threatening trauma forces the captive to identify with and befriend the captor. Ultimately the captive may identify with the captor and develop negative feelings toward the authorities, who represent a danger to both the captive and the captor. The captive's life has become a commodity of exchange that seems to be ignored by the authorities. Both captive and captor are locked into a mutual fate if the negotiation process is unsuccessful.

If a mutual interaction and exchange that is not threatening to the captor occurs, positive bonding can take place. Commonly referred to as the Stockholm Effect, this bonding occurs when individuals closely share space over time during mutual life-threatening crisis and stress. The Stockholm Effect works in the best interests of the captive and can prevent loss of life. Essentially, the captives identify with the captors, the captives develop bad feelings toward the authorities, and the captors develop good feelings toward the captives.

The term was coined in 1973, after a 131-hour bank robbery siege in Stockholm, Sweden. During this incident, captives feared the police and refused to give evidence against the captors. One captive allegedly initiated sexual relations with her captor and continued the relationship after the bank robber's incarceration.

Although there are exceptions to the Stockholm Effect, such as suicidal captors, mentally ill captors, and religious-political-social fanatics, the Stockholm Effect is likely to occur in the event of a captive taking. It clearly illustrates why time is on the side of the captive and why long captive takings can work in the best interest of the captives and authorities.

When an Officer Is Held Captive

Correctional officers who are taken captive may feel uncertain, helpless, humiliated, guilty, and depressed. The officers should remember that help is on the way and that the safe recovery of the captives is the primary concern of authorities. A correctional officer's knowledge and understanding of emergency response plans will help him or her deal with the stressful situation of being a captive.

Correctional officers should make note of their location when taken captive and concentrate on the details and the people involved. Because prosecution of captors will take place after the captive recovery, officers should make mental notes of all unlawful acts and important events or activities. Officers should remain calm and observant and not draw attention to themselves.

They need to remember that time is on their side. To stay calm, officers should take deep breaths and focus on pleasant and positive thoughts. If possible, officers should keep track of time and keep busy. Any form of mental activity and physical activity, such as stretching exercises, push-ups, etc., will help officers stay calm and alert.

After captive officers are recovered, the officers are likely to experience depression, guilt, humiliation, and similar feelings. Officers recovering from the trauma of being involved in a captive taking should seek professional help.

Summary

Captive recovery is one of the main objectives of captive negotiation and emergency response. Good training, practiced emergency response plans, and effective prison management help prevent loss of life.

When inmates clearly understand that taking captives does not result in their release or amnesty, that they can be prosecuted for crimes committed, and that assault will take place if captives are harmed, then institutions can operate more safely.

References

American Correctional Association. 1981. *Riots and disturbances in correctional institutions.* Laurel, Md.: ACA.

Arnold, J., et al. 1980. *Holocaust at New Mexico State Penitentiary.* Lubbock, Tex.: C.F. Boone.

Atkins, B., and H. R. Click. 1972. *Prisons, violence and politics.* Englewood Cliffs, N.J.: Prentice Hall.

Braswell, M., S. Dillingham, and R. Montgomery. 1985. *Prison violence in America.* Anderson Publishing Co.

Cohen, A., et al., eds. 1976. *Prison violence.* Lexington, Mass.: Health Lexington Books.

Destroches, F. J. 1981. *The treatment of hostages in prison riots: Some hypothesis.* Waterloo, Ontario, Canada: Canadian Prison Service, University of Waterloo.

Fox, V. 1972. Prison riots in a democratic society. *Police* 16 (August).

Jenkins, B. 1976. *Hostage survival: Some preliminary observations.* Rand Corporation.

Strentz, T. 1987. A hostage psychological survival guide. *F.B.I. Law Enforcement Bulletin* (November).

Strentz, T. 1979. Law enforcement policy and ego defense of the hostage. *F.B.I. Law Enforcement Bulletin* (April).

Wolk, R. 1973. *How to be a hostage.* New York: New York State Department of Mental Hygiene.

Wolk, R. *Psychoanalytical conceptualization of hostage systems.* New York: New York State Department of Mental Hygiene.

Supervising Special Needs Inmates

By Marianna Nunan

Correctional officers need to know how to identify special needs inmates and understand their medical, physical, and mental conditions. They should also be aware of these inmates' legal rights.

Correctional officers are likely to encounter inmates with needs that are different from those of the general population. Because these needs can complicate the officers' security and supervisory duties, correctional officers need to know how to identify special needs inmates and understand their medical, physical, and mental conditions. They should also be aware of these inmates' legal rights.

Who Are Special Needs Inmates?

Special needs inmates have various types of medical, physical, and mental disabilities. Such disabilities may make some inmates less able to perform tasks that are routine for inmates who are not disabled. The disabilities may be temporary or permanent, newly acquired or lifelong, and the result of an accident, illness, genetic condition, old age, or the criminal act that led to incarceration. Although there is no rigid and universally accepted definition of special needs inmates, this chapter will discuss supervising inmates who have one or more of the following conditions:

Marianna Nunan is an editor for the American Correctional Association's Communications and Publications Division.

This chapter is based on Working with Special Needs Offenders Correspondence Course *(American Correctional Association 1992).*

- medical problems that require some degree of special care
- contagious diseases
- physical disabilities
- mental handicaps
- mental illnesses

Medical Conditions

Correctional officers need to know which inmates have medical conditions requiring special attention. Some of the medical conditions commonly found among inmates include epilepsy, diabetes, cardiovascular disease (which may lead to strokes, heart attacks, etc.), cancer, allergies, asthma, and substance abuse and addiction. Any one of these conditions can lead to emergency situations in which medical assistance should be requested at once.

Although officers are not responsible for medical treatment and placement decisions, they are responsible for contacting medical staff in case of emergencies. Knowing about certain common medical conditions found among inmates helps the officer to respond to emergencies and to recognize a situation that requires understanding and compassion.

The severity of these conditions can determine whether or not inmates participate in routine activities. For example, inmates with epilepsy should not be assigned to work such as painting, which could require them to climb a ladder—a risky situation in the event of a seizure. Inmates' special needs should also be considered when they are assigned to their living units. For example, inmates with arthritis should not be assigned to a top bunk because they may not have the physical flexibility or dexterity required to safely maneuver up to and down from the bunk.

Contagious Diseases

Each communicable disease has its own properties and requires specific precautions and restrictions. AIDS, hepatitis, and tuberculosis are timely examples.

AIDS

Acquired immune deficiency syndrome (AIDS) is caused by the human immunodeficiency virus (HIV), which attacks the body's natural immune system, making it unable to fight off diseases. In fact, many people who die because of AIDS actually die from an opportunistic infection, such as cancer, pneumonia, or tuberculosis.

Some of the early symptoms of AIDS are weight loss, a bad cough, swollen glands, and frequent colds. Because these symptoms are common, many people infected with AIDS don't know they have the disease until they are tested for it.

HIV is transmitted only through direct blood-to-blood or sexual contact. The most common means of transmission are sexual contact, shared intravenous drug needles, tattoos applied with unsterile equipment, and pregnancy. AIDS is not transmitted through the air, inanimate objects, insect bites, casual contact, or saliva.

Given this information, correctional officers are at very low risk in contracting AIDS from infected inmates. Nonetheless, precautions should be taken when cleaning up all blood and body fluid spills and when conducting searches. Officers should be familiar with their facility's policies and procedures on these precautions.

Hepatitis

Hepatitis is a disease that causes infection of the liver. Attacks may last several weeks, and in some cases the attacks recur as a chronic condition. Like AIDS, hepatitis may be transmitted through body fluids, but unlike AIDS, it is rarely fatal. It can be controlled through medication.

Hepatitis A is transmitted primarily through human waste and sometimes through contaminated food or water. Hepatitis B is transmitted through body fluids, such as blood, semen, saliva, and nasal mucous.

Early symptoms of hepatitis include fatigue, diarrhea, and vomiting. In advanced stages, hepatitis can cause serious liver damage.

Because hepatitis is easily transmitted, medical staff may decide to isolate infected inmates. Eating utensils used by those with hepatitis need to be handled separately and sterilized. Infected inmates should never be assigned to or allowed in food preparation or serving areas.

Tuberculosis

Tuberculosis (TB) is another contagious disease common in correctional environments. It is caused by a bacteria that is spread through the air. In open air, ultraviolet rays of the sun kill TB germs quickly, but in enclosed areas with no fresh air supply, the germ is breathed in and travels to the lungs where it remains dormant until the body's immune system is weakened—perhaps by illness, age, fatigue, malnutrition, or alcoholism. At that point, the germ enters the bloodstream and eats away at large areas of the lungs.

Left unattended, active TB results in chronic cough, fever, night sweats, weight loss, fatigue, and eventually death. Fortunately, TB is preventable and curable through prescription drugs. Medical staff will order isolation for inmates with active TB.

Physical Disabilities

Inmates with physical disabilities often face significant challenges in doing even the most simple tasks, like picking a pencil up from the floor or eating a meal. As in the case of inmates with medical problems, inmates' physical disabilities vary in nature and severity; they include loss or impairment of hearing, sight, limb, or mobility or any other significant physical impairment that interferes with an individual's ability to carry out daily duties.

Correctional officers will find that they need to be patient and understanding when inmates' physical disabilities make them slow to respond to instructions or unable to perform certain functions. For example, inmates who are blind may be physically fit and healthy, but may need assistance getting from one place to another. Inmates who are hearing impaired may not respond to instructions if the officer does not speak slowly and face them so they can read lips, use sign language, or write down the instructions.

Despite their special needs, inmates with physical disabilities should be treated as normally as possible. They should be allowed and required to engage in the daily life of the unit—participating in education programs, vocational training, and recreation.

It is important to remember that inmates with physical disabilities are still inmates who need to be supervised with security in mind. Many disabled individuals function with the help of items such as crutches, canes, prostheses, and wheelchairs. These items present security and management concerns in that they may be used as weapons or to conceal contraband.

Correctional officers should use special care and sensitivity when searching these items. Being ordered to remove his or her prosthesis and then having it searched can be humiliating to the inmate. Correctional officers should use care when handling the equipment so as not to damage it. Common courtesy should be exercised, such as placing an inmate's crutches within his or her reach instead of placing them across the room.

Mental Handicaps

The term mental handicap refers to a diminished ability to learn or to adjust to society. It does not refer to diminished moral development, psychological functioning, or perception of reality. Two common types of mental handicaps are mental retardation and learning disabilities.

Mental Retardation

Individuals who are mentally retarded learn at a slower rate than others. Although some may not have the capacity to learn at all, most are capable of normal physical, emotional, and moral development. Interacting with inmates who are mentally retarded may require correctional officers to be more patient and to use deliberate communication techniques, such as slow and careful speech, repetition of concepts, and simple language.

Despite these accommodations, inmates who are mentally retarded should be treated like other inmates. They should be required to participate in unit activities and programming.

93

It should be noted that because inmates who are mentally retarded often display poor judgment and are anxious to please, they may present safety and security concerns. Unknowingly, they may involve themselves in prohibited activity at the encouragement of other inmates. They are also subject to physical and sexual abuse by other inmates.

Learning Disabilities

Like mental retardation, learning disabilities interfere with a person's ability to learn or to process information. However, unlike mental retardation, learning disabilities are not linked to intelligence. Many individuals with learning disabilities have average or above average intelligence.

Because individuals with learning disabilities often conceal their difficulties in processing information, inmates with learning disabilities may not be identified at intake. When interacting with these inmates, correctional officers should give clear instructions and demonstrate whenever possible. They should also be prepared to offer assistance, protection from manipulative inmates, and overall sensitivity to their disability.

Mental Illnesses

Inmates with mental illnesses usually have normal intelligence; their problems lie not in their ability to think, but in their perception of reality. As in any special needs category, the type and severity of mental illness vary from individual to individual.

Correctional officers face not only the challenge of managing inmates who are already diagnosed with mental illness, but also the possibility of encountering inmates who are developing mental illness. The onset of mental illness is gradual and may be indicated by significant changes in mood, behavior, and eating or sleeping patterns.

Although officers are not responsible for diagnosing or specifically treating inmates with mental illness, their close interaction with inmates allows them to spot abnormal behavior. In this case, officers should refer inmates who show signs of mental illness to treatment.

Some types of mental problems found among inmates include the following:

1. **Schizophrenia**—Individuals with schizophrenia experience delusion, move in bizarre or ritualistic ways, and have hallucinations. Schizophrenic inmates may become violent and hurt themselves or others.

2. **Phobia**—A phobic person has an exaggerated fear of something specific—usually something that is not dangerous or threatening to most people. Although there are many types of phobias, claustrophobia—the fear of small, enclosed spaces—may be of particular concern in correctional facilities.

   Hypochondria is a phobia in which individuals believe they are sick most of the time; they usually imagine that they have come down with a serious disease. Inmates with hypochondria may be difficult to handle because they complain constantly and ask to visit the medical unit frequently. Correctional officers must take all inmates' medical complaints seriously, even if they suspect the complaint to be false.

3. **Paranoia**—Paranoid individuals suffer from delusions. They tend to believe that they are being watched, harassed, or targeted by others who want to harm them. The fear of violence is common in correctional facilities. An inmate's fear that other inmates intend to harm him or her may be justified, so correctional officers should take the claim seriously. The officer should ask questions and get the facts, then report the claim to his or her supervisor.

4. **Depression**—Depression is a common mental illness involving feelings of hopelessness and extreme sadness. It can lead to suicidal feelings and suicide attempts. Officers should be alert to emotional or behavioral changes in inmates suffering from depression. Inmates who are suicidal may have mood swings or may start to give away personal belongings. In the case of a suicide attempt, correctional officers should respond according to their facility's policies and procedures. Doing so will enable officers to maintain security and to help the suicidal inmate in the best possible way.

Many mental illnesses can be treated with prescription drugs. Correctional officers must ensure inmates are taking their medications and not hoarding them to sell to other inmates or to attempt suicide with a drug overdose.

Rights of Special Needs Inmates

Special needs inmates have all the general rights afforded to other inmates. These include the right to a safe environment, appropriate treatment, special education, access to programs and resources, and due process. Correctional institutions are obligated to ensure inmates have access to their rights. Correctional officers, because of their direct interaction with inmates, must be aware of the inmates' rights and ensure that they do not inadvertently violate these rights in the course of carrying out their duties.

Right to a Safe Environment

The courts have interpreted the Eighth Amendment of the U.S. Constitution, which forbids the infliction of "cruel and unusual punishment," to mean that inmates have the right to a safe, secure, and humane correctional environment. Consequently, correctional agencies are responsible for inmates' personal safety and well-being. Although this duty to protect applies to all inmates, it is particularly important for special needs inmates.

For instance, physically disabled inmates may be easy victims of stronger, more aggressive peers. Inmates who are mentally retarded can be easily manipulated into becoming accomplices in prohibited activities, such as smuggling or hiding contraband. Correctional officers need to keep in mind the vulnerabilities of special needs inmates.

Right to Appropriate Treatment

The courts have also decided that withholding medical or mental health care is cruel and unusual punishment. Therefore, inmates' rights to appropriate treatment mean their medical needs must not be ignored. Furthermore, inmates' medical services must be comparable to those available to the general public.

Inmates' rights to reasonable and necessary health care mean correctional institutions must provide prompt medical examinations on admission; regular, uninhibited access to trained medical staff; medical services supervised by a licensed physician; access to emergency medical care twenty-four hours a day; access to an accredited hospital; and adequate medical records.

Only appropriately trained health care professionals should decide what health care to provide inmates. Correctional officers or other nonmedical staff should never be allowed to decide if inmates are ill. Officers are responsible for following the institution's policies and procedures for ensuring inmates have access to the medical unit if they request it.

Right to Special Education

Special education is an important issue when providing for special needs inmates. The Individuals with Disabilities Education Act (IDEA) and the Americans with Disabilities Act (ADA) help to define inmates' rights to education.

IDEA says that all persons under age twenty-two are entitled to a free public education and free special education, if they need it. The act stipulates that those under twenty-two must receive initial screening for disabilities, a full evaluation of any disabilities and a determination of the kind of appropriate services, an individual education plan, education in the least restrictive environment, and any related services, such as transportation or access to special equipment.

ADA prohibits discrimination against Americans with physical and mental disabilities; it applies to all inmates, regardless of age. Under this act, eligible persons cannot be "excluded from or denied the benefits of the services, programs, or activities of a public entity." This means that disabled inmates have the right to special education services.

Right to Access to Programs and Services

ADA guarantees disabled inmates the right to equal access to services and programs and also declares the right to physical access to all important areas of the institution. Whenever possible, access to services should not isolate disabled inmates and prevent them from interacting with other inmates. For example, inmates in wheelchairs should have access to the same dining facilities used by other inmates; they should not be served their meals in their cells, away from other inmates.

Special needs inmates have the right to access programs, such as education, vocational training, industries, leisure-time activities, and recreation. Special planning may be required when establishing programs that will be able to accommodate all inmates, including those with special needs. For example, a program that relies heavily on inmates studying written material may need to be adapted for inmates who are blind who could participate if material in braille or a tutor were provided.

Right to Due Process

Special needs inmates, just like other inmates, are entitled to due process—an established set of rules and principles that must be followed in any proceeding that might result in loss of life, liberty, property, or other constitutionally guaranteed rights. In the correctional setting, due process means that if inmates' disabilities prevent them from either understanding or contributing to a disciplinary hearing, they are entitled to assistance. Correctional officers are sometimes asked to assist a special needs inmate, whether it be reading important documents to an inmate who is blind, explaining the proceedings to an inmate who is mentally retarded, or using sign language to communicate with an inmate who is deaf.

Managing Special Needs Inmates

Special needs inmates require specialized care and supervision, depending on the nature and extent of their disabilities. Although these inmates will need individualized treatment, the basic principles for dealing with special needs inmates are the same.

When managing special needs inmates, correctional officers must be attuned to inmates' symptoms. Because officers interact with inmates directly, they are likely to notice symptoms that indicate medical or mental problems. Therefore, it is important for correctional officers to have a basic understanding of common disabilities. More specifically, correctional officers must know how and when to seek help. For this reason, they should be thoroughly familiar with the institution's policies and procedures on medical assistance.

Officers should know enough about a particular inmate's disability to be able to determine if the inmate has a legitimate problem. Furthermore, learning about an inmate's disability allows correctional officers to assist inmates and medical staff.

When considering the vast scope of duties correctional officers must perform, managing special needs inmates occupies a lot of the officers' time and patience. It is important for officers to remember that maintaining a secure, safe, and orderly environment for all inmates means they cannot spend too much time interacting with a single inmate. Inmates dependent on officers to perform basic activities will monopolize the officers' time. Assistance that fosters independence is the key. Rather than doing for inmates, correctional officers should help disabled inmates help themselves.

For example, officers should help inmates who are blind to become familiar and confident in their surroundings by guiding them through areas they are most likely to use. Once inmates know their surroundings, they will be able to get around without as much help. Disabled inmates who learn to function on their own build self-esteem and survival skills.

Effective communication skills are also important when managing special needs inmates. Officers need to listen to inmates. Listening may help to avoid an emergency and will often help bolster a disabled inmate's morale. Effective communication as a management tool includes responding to what inmates are saying. Responding helps inmates feel that someone cares about their problems and will encourage them to talk out, rather than act out.

It is important to keep in mind that special needs inmates are inmates. Regardless of their disability and their need for some special consideration, special needs inmates can be as manipulative, violent, and nasty as any other inmate.

Conclusion

Correctional officers have the difficult job of supervising inmates with a variety of backgrounds and needs. Some inmates have special needs that require correctional officers to respond with special assistance, precautions, understanding, and patience.

Within the general inmate population, special needs inmates must be afforded the same rights as their fellow inmates. Furthermore, they should be given full access to unit activities and programs, allowing them to interact alongside other inmates. Such management promotes self-esteem and responsibility.

Correctional officers should be careful, however, not to let their compassion for special needs inmates foster a relationship where inmates are dependant on them. By helping special needs inmates help themselves, correctional officers are able to spend more time on supervising and managing all the inmates.

Correctional officers must remember that despite special needs inmates' limitations, they are still inmates. By being informed about medical, physical, and mental conditions and well-versed in their facility's policies and procedures, correctional officers can respond appropriately to special needs inmates and avoid being manipulated by them.

Reference

American Correctional Association. 1992. *Working with Special Needs Offenders Correspondence Course.* Laurel, Md.: ACA.

The Correctional Employee and Litigation

By William C. Collins, J.D.

Suits are serious matters and should not be taken lightly. The employee who is sued needs to make prompt contact with legal counsel and work closely with counsel through the defense of the case.

Being sued for actions arising out of the course of employment is, unfortunately, an occupational hazard for those working in corrections. While lawyers who defend these cases are familiar with how litigation works, the defendant-employee often is not. This unfamiliarity may increase the anxiety attached to being sued. Understanding the mechanics of litigation will help reduce the employee's litigation-related anxiety.

Indemnification of Government Employees in Civil Actions

The first concern of the employee named as a defendant in a suit is usually whether he or she will have to pay damages or lawyer fees. Generally, the employee will not have to pay damages or fees.

State Employees

Virtually every state in the country by statute (often known as a Tort Claims Act) has a procedure by which state employees sued

William C. Collins, J.D., is co-editor of Correctional Law Reporter *and a consultant on legal issues in corrections.*

in the line of work are (1) defended by the state attorney general and (2) indemnified for any costs of litigation, including lawyers' fees and damages. Even when a judgment says it is against the defendant personally, the state typically pays the judgment.

Defense/indemnification statutes act much like private insurance policies for employees. However, like insurance policies, they are not absolute. Although exceptions vary from state to state, in general, Tort Claims Acts provide that the state is not under a duty to defend if the actions of the employee were outside the scope of the employee's duties or were not taken in good faith. Sometimes the statutes allow defense of negligent, but not grossly negligent, actions. Thus in one situation, a state refused to defend an employee of a women's prison in a suit that alleged he had fathered the plaintiff's child, who was conceived and born while the plaintiff was an inmate in the institution. After blood tests determined a very strong probability the employee had in fact fathered the child, the state withdrew its defense because impregnating an inmate could not be seen as being within the duties of the defendant-employee.

Some state laws also impose limits on the amounts of damages they will cover or provide that they will not pay punitive damages.

Sexual harassment is an area of law that may have functionally less indemnification protection than other areas. Employees named in sexual harassment claims may be less likely to be defended than if they were named as defendants in inmate civil rights cases.

Employees should determine what protections their state's defense/indemnification statutes provide. Are there specific limitations in its laws? Are its laws interpreted broadly or narrowly in deciding what sorts of actions may be within the scope of employment? If a law is given a narrow, conservative interpretation, fewer suits against employees will be defended than if it is given a broad interpretation.

Employees of Local Government

It is difficult to generalize about the protections provided to employees of local government. Some states may have "little Tort Claims Acts" that provide protection similar to that provided to state employees. Other jurisdictions may carry insurance or are self-insured.

As with state employees, those who work for local government should determine the scope of protection they have from their jurisdiction's insurance or statutory defense/indemnification procedure.

Criminal Actions

In rare cases, criminal actions may be brought against government employees, either by state or federal prosecuting authorities. Defense of these actions by government lawyers, like defense of civil actions, will usually depend on specific statutory authority. If such authority exists, it will usually be more restrictive than Tort Claims Acts. In other words, there would be fewer situations in which the government could defend its employee in a job-related criminal action.

Types of Lawsuits

There are three types of suits commonly encountered by correctional staff:

- Civil Rights actions brought under 42 USC Sec. 1983
- habeas corpus petitions
- tort suits

Civil Rights Actions

Civil Rights suits are the most common type of suit filed by inmates and seen in the prison context. These cases are brought under a federal statute, 42 USC Sec. 1983, passed by Congress in 1871. The statute was passed in response to post-Civil War actions of the Ku Klux Klan and is sometimes known as the Ku Klux Klan Act. The law languished, largely unused, for decades only to be rediscovered in the 1950s, when it became the primary vehicle for suits in the Civil Rights movement in the South. Subsequently, it has been used for all kinds of Civil Rights issues, including those arising in corrections. Civil Rights cases allege that the defendant has in some way violated the federal constitutional or statutory rights of the plaintiff. (Very few, if any, civil rights actions in the corrections context involve federal statutory rights).

Habeas Corpus

In a habeas corpus action, the petitioner claims that he or she is being held in custody illegally, in violation of some constitutional right. A habeas corpus petition often will not relate to anything a correctional employee did or didn't do. The exception to this is where a habeas corpus petition challenges the result of a prison or jail disciplinary hearing or a work release or parole revocation. But usually, a habeas petition will attack an action of the court or agency responsible for the individual being in custody. Habeas corpus petitions name the custodian of the person as the respondent (defendant), therefore the name of the warden of a prison will frequently appear on the pleadings.

Torts

A tort is defined as a civil wrong and arises when there is a violation of some duty that the defendant owes the plaintiff. A classic type of tort case is the suit that arises from the negligent operation of an automobile, in which the negligence of the defendant (the failure to use reasonable care) injures the plaintiff.

Tort actions common in corrections include such issues as the negligent loss of property, failure to protect the inmate from harm, or breaches of other duties of reasonable care correctional staff may owe inmates or others. An increasingly common tort seen in corrections may be medical malpractice actions.

In some states, victims of crimes committed by persons under some form of supervision (probation, parole, etc.) are able to sue supervising officials and agencies under theories of negligence in release or supervision.

Generally for such suits to proceed, the plaintiff must show some sort of special relationship existed between the plaintiff and the state. This relationship might be found where the offender made a specific threat against an identified victim or small, definable class of potential victims and the state failed to warn the victims. Another example would be where the state in some way undertakes the responsibility of protecting the victim and then fails to do so.

How Does a Lawsuit Work?

Summons and Complaint

Generally, the first notice a defendant has that a suit has been filed against him or her is the receipt of a summons and a complaint.

The summons officially notifies the defendant that a suit has been filed and that he or she has a limited period of time (usually twenty or thirty days) in which to respond to (answer) the allegations of the complaint.

The complaint indicates who the plaintiff and defendant are and alleges what the plaintiff contends the defendant did, how that violates the rights of the plaintiff, and what relief the plaintiff seeks.

Different courts have different means of serving a summons and complaint on a defendant. In some cases, the documents may be served by any disinterested person. Federal courts often require that a federal marshal serve the documents, although in some cases service by certified mail is allowed. Generally service by regular mail is not considered effective, because the plaintiff ultimately may have to prove the summons and complaint were served on the defendant.

Employees served documents that appear to be a summons and complaint (or other litigation-related documents) should not attempt to determine the documents' legitimacy. They should immediately notify their lawyers (or at least their supervisors) of receipt of the documents.

Prompt response to a summons and complaint is necessary. Unless an answer or other appropriate documents are filed on behalf of the defendant within the time specified in the summons, a plaintiff can, by proving the documents were served on the defendant, obtain a default judgment from the court. This judgment will award the plaintiff all, or at least a substantial part, of what the complaint asks for without any participation of the defendant whatsoever.

One thing a defendant served with a summons and complaint should *not* do is answer the allegations personally by directly contacting either the plaintiff or the plaintiff's lawyer. The answer called for by the summons is a formal document that, unless properly prepared, may inadvertently prejudice the defendant's defense of the suit in some way. The proper response to a summons and complaint is for the defendant to contact his or her lawyer.

In some situations, a court may dismiss a case before it is even served on a defendant. This may occur only when the inmate is asking the court to waive all filing fees (permission to proceed *in forma pauperis*) and it is clear from the face of the documents the inmate has filed with the court that the complaint is both factually and legally clearly without any merit or substance whatsoever. Courts that have a high volume of inmate cases may hire special law clerks to review inmate cases as they are filed.

The lawyer defending the case will need to get the defendant's version of what happened soon after the complaint is served to be able to file an answer and to begin putting the defense of the case together. It is vital for the lawyer to be advised of all the relevant facts surrounding the allegations. It is common for a complaint to allege facts that tend to support the claim of the lawsuit and to ignore or overlook facts not favorable to the plaintiff's position. Unless the defendant's lawyer knows all the facts, the case may be lost.

Discovery

Under the rules by which suits operate, each side is entitled to attempt to find out virtually all of the facts possessed by the other side prior to the case going to trial. This process is called "discovery." The theory behind discovery is that cases will be settled more readily or justice will be better served through the trial process where each side knows virtually all the facts relevant to the suit, rather than having the suit determined by surprise facts that one side has managed to hide from the other until the trial is under way.

Discovery takes three primary forms: depositions, interrogatories, and motions to produce documents.

A deposition involves a lawyer for one side in a case examining a witness for the other side. The testimony is given under oath before a court reporter, but without a judge present. Depositions of plaintiffs and defendants in suits are very common, and lawyers will generally attempt to depose any and all witnesses the other side proposes to call at trial.

Interrogatories are written questions from one side to the other that the party is required to answer under oath. Interrogatories (often accompanied by requests for admissions to specific facts) generally look for fairly objective sorts of information, including who the witnesses in a case may be.

Motions to produce documents often accompany interrogatories. The interrogatory will ask the party to identify what documents may exist relevant to the controversy, and the motion to produce will request the documents so identified be turned over to the requesting party. When gathering documents to fulfill a formal motion to produce, the client should notify his or her lawyer if any of the documents are confidential and should not be shared with the inmate. In some such cases, the court may allow the documents to be withheld or impose other forms of protection.

Handling discovery requests involves cooperation of lawyer and client. The client should respond to discovery requests only through counsel, but the client may have to do the bulk of the work in responding because the client, not the lawyer, will know what documents exist, where they are, etc.

Techniques to Avoid a Trial

There are two methods commonly used in inmate-filed cases that often result in dismissal of the case in favor of the defendant before trial.

One method is the motion to dismiss. In a motion to dismiss, the defendant says, in essence, "assuming all of the facts alleged by the plaintiff to be true, the plaintiff is still not entitled to any relief because the facts do not show the defendant violated any right of the plaintiff."

As an absurd example, an inmate-plaintiff might allege that his rights were violated because he was not allowed to bring a dozen friends from across the state to the prison at state expense to help him celebrate his birthday. A court would respond to a motion to dismiss in this case by saying, "Even if these facts are true, the state has no legal duty to spend money to help an inmate celebrate his birthday. Therefore, the plaintiff 'fails to state a claim on which relief can be granted' and the defendant's motion to dismiss is granted. Case dismissed."

The second motion frequently used to dispose of cases before trial (and which can be brought by either party) is a motion for summary judgment. When a party can show, through affidavits and other documents, that there are no significant facts at issue between the parties, the moving party is entitled to have the judge decide the case on its merits, i.e., grant a summary judgment. If there is no dispute about the material facts in a case, then there is no need to have a trial, and the judge can apply the law to the facts the parties agree exist.

Trial and Appeal

The trial is the process by which each side presents its case to the trier of fact (the judge or the jury) for determination as to whose version of the facts—the plaintiff's or the defendant's—is the more believable. In a jury case, the jury decides the facts, but is instructed by the judge as to what the law is. The jury then determines if the facts they have found violate the law as it is described to them.

On appeal, no further testimony is taken. Instead, the appellate court reviews the written record from the trial and determines if the law was correctly applied. Except in rare cases, the appellate court is bound by the facts found by the judge or jury because the appellate court isn't able to evaluate the credibility and demeanor of the witnesses who testified at trial.

Testifying

Where there is a trial, there is testimony. Testifying can be a stressful process for a witness, especially when the witness may have important testimony to offer and is not familiar with testifying.

Before a witness testifies, the lawyer presenting the witness should discuss with the witness the issues that will be covered and the questions to be asked. There is nothing wrong with this, and in fact, no good lawyer will put witnesses on the stand without talking to them first. (A saying among lawyers is, "Never ask a witness a question unless you know the answer.") If asked by the opposing lawyer, "Have you discussed your testimony with anyone prior to taking the stand?" the witness should not hesitate to respond, "Yes, I discussed the testimony with my lawyer."

The following are a few suggestions that may help witnesses present testimony in the best possible way:

1. Be familiar with the subject of your testimony before taking the stand. Review your records and notes. Review depositions you gave, because they may have been given months before trial.

2. Dress neatly. Act and appear professional the entire time you are in court, not just while you are on the witness stand. If you wear a uniform, check with your lawyer as to whether you should wear the uniform to court when you testify.

3. Arrive early and let your lawyer know you are present. You may have to wait outside the courtroom before testifying.

4. Don't memorize your testimony. It won't sound natural, and if you forget your "lines," your testimony will be unconvincing.

5. When testifying, speak loudly and clearly. Speak so you can be heard by the farthest juror. Remember to answer questions verbally, not by nodding or shaking your head. Your testimony is being transcribed, and the court reporter can only record verbal answers, not body language.

6. Listen to the question, be sure you understand it before answering, and answer only the question asked. Think about your answer before you give it and avoid giving

snap answers. If you don't understand the question, ask that it be clarified.

7. Don't volunteer additional information. If you feel you have answered the question, stop talking. If the lawyer delays in asking the next question, don't feel obligated to fill the silence with an additional answer.

8. Try to answer questions yes or no or otherwise with short answers. If the lawyer wants only a yes or no answer but you cannot answer with just a yes or no, say so. You should be allowed to explain your answer.

9. Correct answers that you may give in error. It is easier to correct a mistake as it happens than to try to fix it later.

10. You normally will not be allowed to give opinions. Testify just as to the facts, and do not be afraid to say "I don't know" or "I can't remember." Don't exaggerate or try to make up details in an attempt to make your testimony sound better. Stick to what you know.

11. Tell the truth, even it you feel it may damage your case. A lie can hurt the case much more than damaging truth that is readily admitted.

12. Always be courteous. This may not be easy if the lawyer questioning you is hostile. Getting angry with the lawyer or trying to act "smart" with the lawyer will usually work against you.

13. Don't look to the court for help or guidance in answering a question. Your lawyer should object if the question is improper. If no objection is made, you should answer the question. An exception to this is where you are testifying without a lawyer (perhaps introducing records in a dispute between two other parties). In this situation, you may ask the judge about answering, at least to a limited degree.

14. Stop talking when the judge interrupts or an attorney objects to a question. When being cross-examined by the opposing lawyer, it is good practice to pause for a couple of seconds before beginning your answer to allow your lawyer time to make objections.

15. Speak plain English. Avoid technical or informal jargon and acronyms. Using institutional slang ("Then we called the goon squad") may create a negative impression. Remember, your audience (the judge and jury) do not understand corrections.

16. When your testimony is complete, leave the courtroom with a confident expression. Normally, you should not linger in the courtroom (unless, of course, you are a party in the case and attending the entire trial).

Working with Your Lawyer

Lawyers who defend suits are very familiar with the way suits wind their way from summons and complaint through discovery and pretrial motions to trial, appeal, and final decision. Unfortunately, because of this familiarity and heavy workloads they may forget to keep their clients advised of the progress of the suit. Correctional employees who find themselves defendants in a suit should not hesitate to ask their lawyers about the status of their case. Lawyers are obligated to keep their clients informed.

Although it may seem to be a slow, plodding activity to the observer, to the lawyer trying the case, the trial is a very intense time. The court expects the lawyer to be ready to proceed with the case from start to finish without delay. While a witness worries about his or her own testimony, the lawyer may be worrying about the testimony and scheduling of a dozen witnesses, plus a variety of other concerns.

Because of the intensity of the trial and pressure to keep the trial moving, an individual witness may feel he or she is being treated brusquely by the court and even by the lawyer who called the witness. To a large extent, this is simply inevitable, and the witness therefore should not expect to have time to discuss the testimony with the lawyer just before or after the witness is called to testify.

Conclusion

Except in truly rare circumstances, lawsuits against a correctional employee do not threaten the employee's personal finances. Although offenders may file many suits, an overwhelming majority of such suits are resolved in favor of the defendant-correctional employee, usually without even going to trial. It is equally important to recognize that suits are serious matters and should not be taken lightly. The employee who is sued needs to make prompt contact with legal counsel and work closely with counsel through the defense of the case.

Correspondence Courses

A course tailor-made just for you!

❙ Working with Manipulative Inmates ❙

- Motivating Correctional Staff
- Working with Special Needs Offenders
- Correctional Officer
- Correctional Officer II
- Correctional Supervision
- Correctional Supervision II
- Correctional Mid-Management Skills

- Suicide Prevention in Custody – *Intensive Study Course*
- Legal Issues for Correctional Officers
- Legal Issues for Probation and Parole Officers
- Juvenile Careworker
- Correctional Food Service
- Report Writing

Call 1-800-825-2665 for more information or a complete catalog!

Ask about our quantity discounts!

Other Titles

Available from ACA